WHY we get Mental Disorders?

What Pharmaceuticals and Psychiatry will never tell you!

SHUBHAM GUPTA

This book is dedicated to all those who lost their lives in fighting the menace of mental illness

Contents

Preface

"Not being able to talk to anyone because I don't think anyone understands what I was experiencing. I was scared to wakeup. I didn't want to wakeup. I found comfort in sleep because I found that was my escape. Waking up was a struggle. I didn't like the sound of the alarm. I didn't want to face the day." These lines were said by the bollywod superstar Deepika Padukone in an interview to NDTV.

Jim Carrey easily makes the short list of history's most influential comedians, but in an interview with 60 Minutes, the comedian shocked a lot of people when he acknowledged he has spent much of his life dealing with depression. "You need to get out of bed every day and say that life is good. That's what I did, although at times it was very difficult for me," said Carrey.

Mental illnesses are the real deal and here to stay. They have become part and parcel of our lives. Depression is a real problem which science believes is caused by imbalances of certain chemicals in the brain. The situation is really scary when you hear the number of people getting diagnosed with some form of mental disorders.

Not only has the number of patients increased, but the number of mental disorders has also multiplied many times in the last few decades. Now we have around 400 official diagnoses for mental disorders. There are 400 different types of mental disorders! Hoarding is a disorder now. Caffeine withdrawl is a disorder now. Binge eating is a disorder now. Online Gaming addiction is a disorder now.

There are so many disorders now that it will be almost impossible to now not to get labelled with more than 1 sort of mental illness. Depression is one of the major problems in the world. It gives people a feeling of "helplessness", "emptiness", and "directionlessness".

Children are now being diagnosed with ADD, ADHD, Bipolar, GAD (generalized anxiety disorders) and what not. While science is not concerned about the real reasons for these mental issues, this book is. This book is not concerned with what real symptoms are. I am more concerned to explain to you the 'Mind'. Once you understand the basis of the mind, you can understand most mental problems. And once you understand the problem, there is a hope that you might be able to solve it one day.

This book is designed to keep this in mind. The first half of the book talks about psychiatry and its history. You will come to know the level of fraud that has perpetuated in this profession. The second half of the book is designed to take you deep into the mind. Make you realize what and how your mind works! There is a 'WHY' hidden for each and every illness. Illnesses don't happen out of the blue. The science of psychiatry is not concerned about the reasons 'WHY' someone may have bipolar or ADHD or clinical depression. They are only concerned about the symptoms you have. We will discuss facts which psychiatry and pharmaceuticals don't want you to know!

Psychiatrist cannot help you unless you can help yourself. If you really want to help yourself, this book is designed to bring you out of your mind and bring you to life again.

Shubham Gupta

24-02-2019

1. Depression is a disease of the civilized world!

"If it can be solved by $5,000 or a new boyfriend, it's not depression."

-        *– Ned Shorter, Professor of Psychiatry*

It can difficult to define terms like depression or any other mental illnesses like bipolar or ADHD. According to WHO, depression is a common mental disorder and globally more than 300 million people of all ages suffer from it. If we go by the literal meaning of depression, it is a close synonym to prolonged sadness. Depression is a mental state which is a combination of negative thoughts, anxiety, and hopelessness. A person who is depressed has lost the ability to feel, think and act. There is always fear and uncertainty of the future. Depression impairs your ability to think because there is an inner feeling that whatever you do, it will not make the situation any better.

They're talented, attractive, wealthy, and widely acclaimed. But neither fame nor fortune immunizes celebrities against the ravages of depression and mood disorders. Today, when a celebrity's missteps can "break the Internet," says Vasilis K. Pozios, MD, a forensic psychiatrist, the resulting public scrutiny can provoke feelings of guilt, shame, and insecurity.

Linkin Park lead singer Chester Bennington killed himself. He had everything anyone would aspire. The 41-year-old had struggled throughout his life with drugs and alcohol and the trauma of child abuse. Bennington had previously spoken about having suicidal thoughts after his marriage fell apart with the first wife in 2005.

What's more, celebrities often experience key risk factors for depression, including substance abuse, sleep disruption, unemployment, and highly variable work schedules, says Scott A. Langenecker Ph.D. associate professor of psychiatry. "Some celebrities struggle to balance their public and private lives. Their self-esteem may not necessarily be built upon their authentic self, and so may be fragile and contingent upon continued fame," says Dr. Pozios. [1]

War veterans suffer depression once they come back to their homes. Students can suffer depression if they failed an exam. Professionals can get into this emotional trauma if they are about to get a pink slip. A person can fall in depression if they fall out of a marriage. A person who has been diagnosed with a terminal illness can also get into depression. Children can get into depression due to constant bullying or body shaming. Depression is a direct result of things going out of our hands. Depression occurs when we find ourselves incapable of coming out of a life situation; where we don't see any light at the end of the tunnel.

Sometimes a sense of realization can come that your life is useless and meaningless. You might be working in some place and you suddenly realize what irrelevant thing you are doing. It is not satisfying the real you. You might be trying to imitate someone. You might be doing something which you don't love. You are simply doing it for money. There is a sense of sadness and dissatisfaction. People can also call this as depression.

Depression is generally a reaction of our body when we are helpless. Suicide is an extreme form of depression. When the only way out of the present misery is to die, depression can become extreme. Let's all understand that depression or anxiety is a direct outcome of an external situation. When we are anxious about the future, we go into depression. We don't become anxious or depressed without any reason. Do you agree?

I know some of you might be saying NO. I know that you have been constantly told that depression or any other mental disorder is a result of a brain dysfunction and hence you don't need a reason to be depressed. Also depression or any other mental disorder can be blamed directly to the genes you got and hence you cannot treat it. It's part of you! I am not saying that these theories are wrong but if you can stick around, we can relook at these theories in the coming chapters.

Depression has to have an external cause. See a 6-month old child. Unless already diagnosed with some disease, you will find the kid full of life and happiness. He or she can smile all day for no big reason. Depression is not the emotion which a kid exudes. Look at the 1-year-olds, they are running around the house. They are so happy. There is no depression. You will not see them sitting bored in the room.

Imagine your colleague comes to the office and says, "I am really depressed today!" What will be your reaction? The obvious reaction will be, "what happened?" Is it not?

In our lifetime, most all of us have had faced an episode of depression. It is often normal human reactions to life challenges and pressures ex: divorces, break-ups, sexual or psychological abuse, and loss of loved ones.

Even our economy also falls into depression from time to time. The great depression happened in 1929. In economics, a depression is sustained, long term downturn in economic activity in one or more economies. We argued earlier that for any reaction, there must be an equal and opposite reaction. There is always a reason for the economic recession. It can be wars, lack of available credit due to mass loan defaults among many others.

But there is always a reason why there is an economic recession. Economic depression doesn't happen out of the blue. Similar goes true with the depression in humans.

Now come to medical science. Here depression is referred as clinical depression. Clinical death means that a death pronounced in a hospital by a doctor. Similarly, depression pronoun by a psychiatrist inside a hospital is called clinical depression. According to American psychiatric association, depression is defined as "Depression (major depressive disorder) is a common and serious medical illness that negatively affects how you feel the way you think and how you act. Depression causes feelings of sadness and/or a loss of interest in activities once enjoyed. It can lead to a variety of emotional and physical problems and can decrease a person's ability to function at work and at home."

Depression symptoms can vary from mild to severe and can include:

1. Feeling sad or having a depressed mood

2. Loss of interest or pleasure in activities once enjoyed

3. Changes in appetite — weight loss or gain unrelated to dieting

4. Trouble sleeping or sleeping too much

5.   Loss of energy or increased fatigue

6.   Increase in purposeless physical activity (e.g., hand-wringing or pacing) or slowed movements and speech (actions observable by others)

7.   Feeling worthless or guilty

8.   Difficulty thinking, concentrating or making decisions

9.   Thoughts of death or suicide

If we look closely at all the symptoms of clinical depression, you can realize that they seem all right. If you having relationship issues like divorce or losing your job, feeling sad, worthless, fatigue, loss of interest in things you loved earlier, loss of appetite will be a direct outcome. You will have trouble sleeping. You will not find an interest in life. You might experience irritability, anxiety and reduced interest. You will be always worried about the future. All these can be a normal outcome for a person who is facing a dramatic life event.

There is also a possibility that you might face some of these symptoms without any dramatic life event. For example children facing bullying or body shaming in schools or you are facing undue pressures in the workplace. From the surface, the life of such a person may look ok but inside the mind, there is a struggle going on every day.

The American Psychiatric Association (APA) argues that sadness due to the death of a loved one, loss of a job or the ending of a relationship is difficult experiences for a person to endure but cannot be called depression. Here is the argument which the association makes:

Sometimes people become depressed for what seems like a good reason—maybe they lost their job or a close friend passed away—but with clinical depression, there doesn't necessarily have to be a reason for how you feel. The chemicals in the brain which are responsible for mood control may be out of balance causing you to feel bad even though everything in your life is going well.

APA says that in grief self-esteem is not lost but in depression, you tend to have low self-esteem. Does this argument make sense?

If I lose my job, will it not hit my self-esteem? Isn't it saying that I am not good enough? It is a direct hit on to a person's self-worth. A divorce can hit a person's self-worth. It might give a feeling that they are not good enough. Love is the greatest emotion that we all crave for. Losing a loved one can give a feeling that you will never get the love you desire. Diagnosis of diseases like HIV, cancer, and diabetes can also trigger a feeling of low self-worth. Bullying and body-shaming can seriously affect the way you perceive your self-worth.

We can argue over these points but net-net is that there is no clear demarcation between what can be depression and what can be grief. Some people can better manage grief while some are not able to handle even the slightest of negative situation. Lot of this has to be dependent on how you were raised as a kid. We will understand more about mind in future chapters.

Apart from sadness and grief, psychology and psychiatry also blame genetics and chemical imbalance in the brain as new age reasons for mental illnesses. This indirectly means that you can be depressed without any reason at all. You don't need a reason or occasion to be depressed. It's like flu which you can get on any day.

Let me ask you: what should be the best way to treat depression of a person? According to psychiatry, depression can be **managed** in below ways:

1. Medication: The premise behind this treatment is that since there is a chemical imbalance in the brain, it can be corrected by chemical balancers. Psychiatrists usually recommend that patients continue to take medication for six or more months after symptoms have improved. Longer-term maintenance treatment may be suggested to decrease the risk of future episodes for certain people at high risk.

2. Psychotherapy: Social support, Cognitive behavioural therapy (CBT) and interpersonal psychotherapy are considered the best way to treat a person. Cognitive behavioural therapy (CBT) has been found to be effective in treating depression. CBT is a form of therapy focused on the present and problem solving. CBT helps a person to recognize distorted thinking and then change behaviours and thinking. Psychotherapy may involve only the individual, but it can include others. For example, family or couples therapy can help address issues within these close relationships. Group therapy involves people with similar illnesses.

3. Electroconvulsive Therapy (ECT): This is a medical treatment most commonly used for patients with severe major depression. You must have seen old movies, where mentally troubled people are given shocks to calm them down. This is the modern version of the same therapy.

Many young people are now claiming that they are depressed. They are clueless about life and what is the meaning. Many people are now calling depression as a disease of the civilized world. Depression is an outcome of living a life driven by materialism.

In the next few chapters, we will really deep dive into the world of psychiatry and try to understand why depression is labelled as a disease.

15

2. History of Psychiatry

In the present world, there is a buzz about mental disorders including depression. Psychiatrists claim that over 1 billion of the population of the world is mentally ill. In India, we are now seeing television advertisements about depression which I have never seen before. Some speakers call it a disease of the civilized world. From where are all the mental illnesses including depression coming from? Without understanding the history of mental illness, it will be very difficult to understand the 'WHY' of mental illnesses.

This part might come to most of you as a shock. Psychiatry has a very troubling genesis. This is a field where there is a lot of controversy throughout. Look at what many renowned psychiatrists have to say about their own field and its development:

"There is not one shred of credible evidence that any respectable scientist would consider valid demonstrating that anything that psychiatrist call mental illness is brain diseases or biochemical imbalances. It's all fraud," said Dr. Ron Leifer.

"There is no reliability of diagnosis and there is no science. It's just pseudoscience. Its pretence science," said Dr. Margaret Hagen.

Dr. Gary Null said, "This is one of the most open secrets in all of America in the psychiatric field that nothing that is being done is legitimate and they are billing for it."

Dr. Jock McLaren is an Australian psychiatrist who worked 25yrs in the remote north of the country. He occupies himself delving into the philosophical basis of psychiatry, only to find there isn't one. He said, "What's happening in psychiatry is that there is a general agreement there will be no criticism of the status quo. There will be no criticism."

Dr. Thomas Szasz said, "Chemical imbalance meshes very well with a chemical which can balance the imbalance. It's mythology. It's a fable. That is the baselines of which we are operating."

So, what is wrong with psychiatry? Why is their own revolting against their practices? To truly understand this, we need to go back into history.

In the past four decades (1965 -2005), twice as many people have died in the US government psychiatric hospital than in all US wars since 1776. The number of death has been more than 1.1 million. Insurance companies pay-out nearly 70 billion dollars every year for psychiatric services doubling the cost of medical insurance premiums.

"The roots of psychiatry have to do with power, control, and alienation from certain groups of people who were uncomfortable to be around. They were locked up in these places to get them out of the way," said Dr. Lee Coleman.

The history of psychiatry is really to do with institutions called mental asylums. Bethlehem Royal Hospital in London was among the world's first psychiatric institutions. It was a place to keep the people who were called mad. Inmates were confined in closet, cages and chained to walls. In the 18th century there was a slight shift. From storing and torturing the mentally ill, psychiatrists decided to start treating the mentally ill.

William Battie (1703 -1776) was an English physician who published in 1758 the first lengthy book on the treatment of mental illness. The book was called *A Treatise on Madness*. By extending methods of treatment to the poor as well as the affluent, Battie helped raise psychiatry to a respectable specialty. Prior to his work, psychiatry was considered only as caretakers of the mentally ill. They were not really considered as "real" doctors.

William Battie was the President of the Royal College of Physicians in 1764. He started promoting that his new mental asylum can better manage and even actually cure madness. His mad houses made him among the richest man in England, though his treatments were every bit inhumane.

Although Battie made claims that he could heal people, he didn't heal even a single patient. But he anyways succeeded. His success triggered a boom in the asylum business and psychiatrists to cash in this new business. Any means were used which would calm down a patient and many of these so-called treatments were torture. The near drowning devices were invented during that period. A patient was put in a coffin and the closed coffin then was lowered into the water. After a few seconds of drowning, the patient was pulled out. There is no need to guess that the mortality rates in such treatments were very high.

To make the psychiatric treatment more scientific and reliable, there was a push to promote a biological theory of medical treatment. An American physician Benjamin Rush (1746-1813) put forth the idea that insanity was caused by too much blood in the head. The cure would be any way which will remove that excess blood from the head of a mad person.

In 1792, Rush read a paper before the American Philosophical Society which argued that the "color" and "figure" of blacks were derived from a form of leprosy. He argued that with proper treatment, blacks could be cured and become white. [1]

He invented many devices which would drain blood from the body. These included bloodletting. Rush would bleed their patients till they became less psychotic. He also invented the tranquilizer chair where the patient was tied on to a chair and cold water was poured into his head. This process was carried on for hours. His lethal ways of treatment were outlined in his book and remained psychiatry's authoritative text for the next 70 years.

Rush was so revered that in 1965, he was enshrined as the father of American psychiatry. Imagine the father of psychiatry is a person who had no clue of what mental illness was!

By the 1800s, it was getting evident that psychiatry was a failure in treating madness. The cures promised weren't delivered so by the 1860s a growing mood of pessimism was growing over the whole west that the psychiatric institutions were ever growing in size but not growing in their effectiveness. This started threatening the financial bottom line of most psychiatric practices. Soon the whole science was being pushed to invent new medical models.

The 20th century brought more medical models. American psychiatrist Henry Cotton mutilated his patients by removing their body parts. He declared this procedure as a **medical breakthrough** in the treatment of mental illness. Henry believed that mental illness was called by certain body parts. Doctors would remove the teeth, tonsils, stomach, spleen and other body parts of the mentally ill. Obviously, public outcry happened over the barbaric torturing of patients and they have to reinvent another treatment.

"This is the history of psychiatry more or less to damage the patient. This was another model to chain them like animals," said Dr. Thomas Szasz.

Really what psychiatry has done is to torture the patients in whatever ways it wanted. The psychiatry continued to gain legitimacy by reshaping them as a medical discipline. Psychiatry carried a legacy of torture and death. Presently they are running their most profitable model of all time; the mass drugging of the millions.

In the late 1800s, German professor Wilhelm Wundt declared that men's personality, behaviour, thoughts are nothing more than chemical reactions in the brain. Wundt became frustrated with his inability to change behaviour because he was initially dealing with the logic of a soul. He created a new science which was based on a logic that man is an animal without a soul. Man needs to be trained like a horse or a dog. He should not be a thinker.

This new definition of man as a soulless organism was soon studied by students from across the world. Following Wundt theory, Russian scientist Ivan Pavlov conducted the famous animal experiments. We all must have studied his experiments with dogs using a bell.

During the 1890s, Russian physiologist, Ivan Pavlov was researching salivation in dogs in response to being fed. He inserted a small test tube into the cheek of each dog to measure saliva when the dogs were fed.

Pavlov predicted the dogs would salivate in response to the food placed in front of them, but he noticed that his dogs would begin to salivate whenever they heard the footsteps of his assistant who was bringing them the food. Later this experiment was replaced by a bell sound post which the food was served. He called this conditional reflex. The dogs would salivate just by a ringing of the bell. This gave the indication to Pavlov that we can condition the responses of a living being through proper training.

Later he tried replicating the same experiment on children. He punctured holes in their cheeks to collect and measure the amount of saliva. Pavlov's conditioning became one of the major foundations of a lot of behavioural science research in the 20th century. The idea that man is an animal whose behaviour can or should be controlled became the dominant idea. Nobody wanted a thinking man. Authority definitely didn't want a thinking man. A thinking man is dangerous. Psychologists started targeting children as children can be trained easily.

The idea that behaviour can be conditioned by repetition was called **behaviourism**. Dr. Samuel Blumenfeld said, "Behaviourists believed that all children are animals and can be trained like animals. Psychologist James Watson, the most famous of the behaviourist said that you have to look at human beings as you look at the ox you slaughter. Behaviourist doesn't believe there is a soul."

Watson successor was a Harvard psychologist named B. F. Skinner. Skinner considered free will an illusion and human action dependent on the consequences of previous actions. Skinner was able to demonstrate that animal behaviour can be changed by certain reinforcements. If the consequences are bad, there is a high chance the action will not be repeated; if the consequences are good, the probability of the action being repeated becomes stronger. Skinner called this the principle of reinforcement.

He could teach pigeons to play ping pong, rats to run mazes, humans to any end based on economical or material rewards. Skinner was actually able to shape new behaviour patterns. He soon became very famous for his ideas. Skinner's views influenced education as well as psychology.

The idea was mostly that human behaviour can be conditioned similarly to that of animals like a rat.

Still, 40 million dollars of taxpayer money is being paid by United States National institute of mental health for behavioural psychology research which makes it total 20 billion dollars since 1948. With these funds, psychology applies the same conditioning techniques developed by Pavlov and Skinner.

Aversion therapy is a form of behaviour therapy in which an aversive (causing a strong feeling of dislike or disgust) stimulus is paired with undesirable behaviour in order to reduce or eliminate that behaviour. People were shocked to respond in a certain way. If they revolted, they were shocked and tortured. Any way was used to increase man's submission.

The idea to control people's behaviour and personalities became a dominant force in psychiatry. In the same period, a psychologist named Francis Galton (1822-1911) worked on a new theory called Eugenics. Eugenics, by the way, is no more considered a science. The Darwin's idea of natural selection was too random for people and they wanted to take control of this selection process in their own hands.

Eugenics believed that human beings should take evolution in their own hands. Galton believed in the idea of the gene pool of the human species can somehow be improved if certain people with different abilities (including mentally ill) didn't have kids. The belief was that if the people with good genes (people who are most talented, most attractive, most healthy) were producing more, we can improve the human race else we are going downhill as a society. The major concern behind Eugenics was that the people who were supposedly had poor genes were reproducing faster.

From where can someone come up with this stupid idea? Of course from the works of his half-cousin, Charles Darwin.

This idea soon got tractions from the nobles. It was observed that the esteemed and genius members of the society often married late and had fewer children while the inferior people including the poor, weak or simply different reproduced more. Francis wanted the families of merit to grow and the families of the weak (remember the concept of survival of the fittest) should be stopped from reproducing. Also, he noticed that the hereditary traits become weaker if a high-class individual marries a lower class member. This might mean that the children of such mixed couples might lose royalty and genius.

He was the first to apply statistical methods to the study of human differences and inheritance of intelligence and introduced the use of questionnaires and surveys for collecting data on human communities, which he needed for genealogical and biographical works and for his anthropometric studies.

After the death of Galton in 1911, the eugenics caught traction in many countries including the United States. In fact, the countries started passing Eugenics laws which included forced sterilization laws. Driven by fear that births of supposedly inferior people would lead to weak or criminally "degenerate" adults, some states introduced forcible vasectomy of already incarcerated groups and those with different abilities. In fact, it was now no more science or genetics but more of anybody "we don't like" were forced to stop reproduction by force.

This work also became the logic behind intelligence scale which is commonly known as IQ. The basis was to avoid a low IQ person marry a high IQ since the offspring will be weaker. The IQ tests were also used to place people in different roles for example roles in the army. The aptitude tests were designed to place soldiers in different roles. This act of segregating human beings based on quantitative mechanisms is still visible in our schools. The children are judged as better based on how well they perform in tests. The children get better colleges and schools based on how well they can remember. This segregation is still visible in our everyday life. The segregation works if the comparison is apple to apple but humans are neither designed like apples nor like rats. People are different. No single human being has the same fingerprint. They are not meant to be the same as well. But the science of one man was soon going to create such massive repercussions, that which no one could have imagined.

This theory was also responsible behind the divide between the black and white and the theory that whites are a superior race and that blacks are inferior. So inferior that they should be slaves to whites. A lawyer named Madison Grant wrote a book called *Passing of the great race* which examined the European ethnic groups such as the Alpine and Nordic races. Below are some of the quotes from his book:

"The intelligence and ability of a coloured person are in pretty direct proportion to the amount of white blood he has, and ... most of the positions of leadership, influence, and prominence in the Negro race are held not by real Negroes but by Mulattoes, many of whom have very little Negro blood."

"No doubt the Mexican Indian is well suited to his environment, and his traditional habits are well suited to him. This does not mean, however, that either has any important contribution to make to the United States which would be realized by a northward mass migration of agricultural and industrial serfs. On the contrary, the Mexican immigration to the United States, which is made up overwhelmingly of the poorer Indian element, has brought nothing but disadvantages."

"Hindu immigration has so far been nothing more than a threat. The present immigration restrictions will prevent the immigration of these people, except for travel and study. Experience in many parts of the world has shown the folly of allowing white countries to be overrun by Hindus, and Americans should sympathize with the British possessions that are trying to maintain white supremacy in their own borders in this respect."

"Where the environment is too soft and luxurious and no strife is required for survival, not only are weak strains and individuals allowed to survive and encouraged to breed but the strong types also grow fat mentally and physically."

"In the democratic forms of government, the operation of universal suffrage tends toward the selection of the average man for public office rather than the man qualified by birth, education, and integrity. From a racial point of view, it will inevitably increase the preponderance of the lower types and cause a corresponding loss of efficiency in the community as a whole."

Read all the above quotes of this man and regret. This man gave all the above logics citing Galton.

Charles Davenport was another zoologist who collected data to help people check whether a potential marriage was suitable.

A nurse named ***Margaret Sanger*** coined the term birth control and she opened a first birth control clinic in the US in 1916. Sanger used the Eugenics to gain legitimacy in her movement. Eugenics became a dominant theme at her birth control seminars and she publicly claimed that there should be an end to the breeding of the "UNFIT".

By the late 1920s, Eugenics was recognized as a bad science by most practicing biologists. But as a source of policy for many lawmakers in the United States, Germany, and elsewhere, Eugenics was still very much alive. The elite and the governments wanted to understand their people and also to shape them.

The Eugenics movement in Germany was taking a completely different shape. Hitler was one of the greatest admirers of the American Eugenicist Madison Grant. Grant's book *The Passing of the Great Race* was proclaimed by Hitler as his personal bible. If you have read the autobiography of Hitler you must have noticed his dislike of Jews from early childhood. This dislike soon became hatred when he was in his 20s. In his book Mein Kampf, Hitler also hailed Eugenics that would rebuild the great old German nation.

"He who is not healthy bodily or mentally is not allowed to perpetuate his malady in the body of his child. The right of personal freedom recedes before his duty to preserve the race," said Adolf Hitler.

The German Eugenicists welcomed the Nazi regime because the Nazi's programs would fund the very programs they had in mind. The Nazis gave them political and financial support and in return, the psychiatrist gave them the medical justification for the genocidal policies.

Dr. Craig Newnes said, "40% of the German psychiatrists willingly joined the Hitler's SS organisation by 1933. They weren't forced to the SS. They just joined that naturally because the beliefs were very very similar. Soon the decision from sterilization moved to murder.

The plan was simple:

1. Convince the public that feeble minded undesirables wanted to escape the burden of their existence but couldn't say or do it. Killing such people is an act of mercy.

2. Extend the definition of inferiors to include anyone we don't like including Jews, Hippies, homosexuals, and witnesses as unworthy of life.

Psychiatrists produced propaganda movies popularly known as Nazi's killing films shown in all 5000 plus theatres throughout Germany.

Dr. Michael Berenbaum, who is a Holocaust scholar, said, "It first started with passive violence which is starvation which then intensified to lethal injections and finally it developed into systematic gassing and cremation."

The psychiatric headquarters were established in Berlin under the infamous name - T4. In this center, 70,000 human beings were killed who were considered as 'life unworthy' which included mentally retarded and disabled. The killing piloted in psychiatric institutions moved from such centres into the concentration camps with the top German psychiatrists as the executioners.

Paul Nitsche, professor of psychiatry and the director at T4 claimed, "The screening in concentration camps went along the same lines and with the same registration forms as in the insane asylums."

60, 00,000 Jews died in this extermination policy. The famous German psychiatrist Ernst Rudin congratulated Hitler for making his 30-year-old dream come true.

After the Nazi regime ended, these German psychiatrists who were directly responsible for the murder of 11 million people quietly settled across different parts of the civilized world and only a handful got a prison sentence for all the war crimes.

The racism that we all talk about so often was the brainchild of psychiatry. In fact, racism in inseparable from the roots of psychiatry. All the racism against the blacks/negroes have a basis in the Eugenics and psychiatry of the 1800s. The Negroes were medically considered diseased and it was necessary for whites to remain separated from them as this will stop the disease to spread to the whites. This mentality of blacks or dark-skinned people being inferior to the whites can still be seen around the world.

Dr. Samuel Cartwright declared that blacks have a mental disorder if they had a desire to run away from slavery. Running away from slavery became such a common problem for whites that psychiatrist named this as a disease. The Psychiatrists also gave a cure for that: lashes on the bareback.

After slavery was abolished, the psychiatric racism didn't end. The American journal of Psychiatry claimed that blacks are the descendants of animals and cannibals and are ill prepared for civilization.

The architect of the Apartheid movement in South Africa was also Eugenics. Dr. Hendrik Verwoerd was the prime minister of South Africa. The prime minister had studied Eugenics as a psychology student in Nazi influenced Germany in the 1920s. He is remembered as an architect of Apartheid. During his regime, blacks had literally no rights whatsoever.

Apartheid not only meant separate and inferior public services, benches and building entrances for non-whites. It also stripped South African blacks of their citizenship. Very similar behaviour was done to the Indians when the British were ruling them. The signboards like 'dogs and Indians not allowed' were common during that racist era. The color of the skin was the basis of superiority and the whites had psychiatry to support their acts.

The blacks were put in mental camps across South Africa. The camps were forced labour houses for cheap labour. By the time the scam was exposed, 70,000 blacks died in these camps and psychiatrist made 117 million dollars in funding from the South African government. In 1983, WHO issued a report which blamed psychiatry to have cultivated racism and Apartheid did have a parallel in the ownership and trading of slaves.

In 1971, psychiatrist Dr. Louis Jolly West continued psychiatric racist agenda by conducting a secret aversion therapy experiment called the violence center. This was a government funded program to implant electrode in the brains of African American and Hispanic males to shock them if they exhibit any violent behaviour and if that didn't work, chemically castrate them with drugs.

In 1994, psychologist Richard Herrnstein co-authored a book called *The Bell Curve*, claiming to prove that blacks were genetically disabled and therefore inferior to whites.

Bell Curve talks about the old Eugenics idea that people are born with different kinds of intellectual abilities. This goes back to the belief that genetically black are inferior to whites. Despite criticism, psychiatry continued their racist theories and agenda.

Politics and psychiatry were a good duo. Psychiatry helped politics in suppressing Dissent. Political repression was supported by psychiatry.

Psychiatric treatments have always been used as a political weapon to control the masses. From Hitler to the Soviet regime, all demanded absolute loyalty towards the state. If anybody whispered their opinion against the regime, they were treated as dissident and put into one of the special psychiatric hospitals.

Soviets have been experts on incarcerating their political dissidents. They would send them to concentration camps in Arctic Circle, where they would work to death. In many cases, they would put them in psychiatric wards and punish them with drugs and electric shocks. China is another totalitarian government which uses similar methods very effectively. Muslim women and children are picked up from their homes and put in one of the concentration camps. Anyone who is seen talking to a foreigner in a public place in China could be held for questioning. Individual freedom is going down and government power is going up all thanks to psychiatry.

According to Soviet psychiatrist, all the dissidents suffered from the inflexibility of conviction, a symptom of a new disorder - sluggish schizophrenia. Like their counterparts in other countries, Soviet psychiatrist also prescribed powerful drugs to treat their patients.

Resisting treatment was also made a disease. From 1967 to 1987, the Soviet government arrested over 2 million people who for political reasons were diagnosed as mentally ill. Even today psychiatry remains a coercive tool of choice for governments throughout the world.

The history of bringing chemical medicines into treating mentally ill was not that great either. The idea was to bring the patient in a docile state with least effort as possible. In the 1920s, psychologist Manfred Sakel declared that there are *bad* brain cells and there are *good* brain cells. Somehow if you give people enough INSULIN, you can kill the bad brain cells. Soon insulin wards became famous around psychiatric hospitals and it became a big business.

Another Hungarian psychiatrist believed he could cure mental illness by inducing brain-damaging seizures with a drug called Metrozol.

In a single day, a doctor could mentally shock 50 patients to bring them to a docile and manageable state. By 1939, Metrozol was used in 70% of the hospitals in America and almost every other country in the world.

The financial success of Insulin and Metrozol sparked the development of even more profitable venture of electrically shocking the patients by brain-damaging convulsions. In Italy 1938, two Italian psychiatrists observed that before slaughtering pigs, in order to make pigs more docile, they would apply electrodes to their temples that was hooked up to wall current. This stunned the pigs but didn't kill them. They can then easily slaughter them. This gave them an idea to try electricity for convulsion therapy. By electrically shock patients, they can bring them easily under control.

Soon this treatment drew a lot of criticism as patients were seen to have an unparalleled agony during those shocks. There were patients with broken bones, spines, teeth after the treatment.

Having sold successfully brain damage as a cure, this went even further. Portuguese neurologist, Egas Moniz tried to change personality by drilling into the patients' skull and pouring pure alcohol directly into the brain, killing the tissues of the frontal lobe. Moniz called this new procedure Lobotomy.

Dr. Walter J. Freeman who was a Lobotomy practitioner, found a faster way, without having to drill the skull of the patient. He would simply lift up the eye of the patient and try to damage the frontal lobe of the patient.

By the time his license was revoked when his last patient died on the operating table, Freeman had performed or supervised 3500 Lobotomy. There was no anaesthesia, mind you. The stories of miraculous cures were soon exposed as brain damaging frauds.

On the criticism of Lobotomy, the psychiatrist brought back the electric shock therapy renaming it as electroconvulsive theory (ECT). They now gave patients anaesthesia and then shock them. A patient is no more crying in pain on the table. This shock therapy is still prescribed to patients as a cure to mental illness.

Half of ECT patients are elderly. Once they become eligible for government healthcare at the age 65, 360% more American receives ECT then at age 64. This added up to 40,000 dead and countless others so brain damaged they have no hope of ever recovering. For electricity worth few dollars, psychiatrist rake in over 5 billion dollars just from the US alone.

The next miracle cure added to their arsenal was more deadly than ever before. This was faster and cheaper and could turn every woman, man and child patients for life. By 1950s, psychiatrist discovered their next miracle cure. A chemical (Thorazine) originally designed to cure parasite in pigs, their new discovery hindered human brain functioning in a much more refined way but much the same way of shoving the eyes prick, inside the eye socket. It was an old treatment in a new disguise. **Thorazine** provided psychiatry an entry into mainstream medicine.

This concept of a pill was a much more efficient way to manage and treat more patients. A patient can come in and within 15 minutes he or she can walk out. This was easy and mess free. The psychiatrists didn't tell the public that Thorazine caused a neurological condition called tardive dyskinesia: a condition affecting the nervous system often caused by long-term use of some psychiatric drugs.

Even if you remove the drug, the side effects persist which is a direct confirmation that the brain has been permanently damaged. The manufacturer of Thorazine made 300% more profits compared to their investment cost. It was only 20 years later that the patients were warned of its side effects.

Soon psychiatry became an industry of drug pushers. The pharma saw this as a good opportunity to expand their reach and target more patients. Pharma started funding the American Psychiatric Association by giving advertisements in APA's official journals. Scientists and researchers were getting more money from pharma then their actual salary.

There was so much money to be made that the entire psychiatrist needed was a scientific theory to justify it. Their solution was to publish an official report declaring that all mental problems derived from so called *chemical imbalance* in the brain requiring drugs to correct. Dr. Mark Filidei said, "Chemical imbalance is one of the greatest fallacies ever foisted upon patients and the public. There is no chemical test to show an imbalance related any psychiatric diseases including depression and anxiety."

Dr. Bob Johnson is the author of the book *Unsafe at any Dose*. He said, "The chemical imbalance is for the benefit of the psychiatrist. It must be there so that psychiatry can treat it."

Soon Pharma, FDA, and Psychiatry were in bed together. The relationship was of purely of benefit. There was no importance to treatments or what was good for the patients. The medical education was influenced. The researchers and scientists were funded and their allegiance was bought. Hundred million have taken Psychiatric drugs backed by fake science and endorsed by regulators who are bought and paid for. Their harmful medication makes pharma over 350 billion dollars a year!!

The mental institutions need patients. In fact, any hospital needs patients to run. It's funny that when we go to a real doctor, we have an option to refuse the prescribed treatment. No doctor can force or imprison us against our wishes but psychiatrists are a different breed. They have *involuntary commitment*. They want to decide what's best for you. You can be taken against your wishes just by a simple nod from Psychiatry.

The large scale idea was a profitable way to keep their million acre Psychiatric institutions filled up. The person who has committed no crime, has faced no trail is sent directly to a mental hospital which is really a prison and a torture house. Even children can be taken away from their parents with little legal recourse.

Psychiatric staffs provoke their patients into violence so that they can take from insurance companies up to 1600 dollars a day for each **restrained** patient.

This burden comes directly to the public in form of soaring health insurance premiums.

Dr. Jeffrey Schaler is a professor at the department of Justice and law, American University. He said, "Involuntary commitment is a form of Psychiatric slavery where persons are treated as if they are property and they are deprived of liberty and any legal rights. And people are making money in the process."

It is said that every 75 sec, somebody in America is committed to a Psychiatric ward against their will. Psychiatrists have earned over $1 trillion since 1965.

R. Christopher Barden is an attorney. He said, "We see that most of the victims of recovered memory therapy were women who had excellent insurance whether it was government or private insurance. Because many insurance policies wouldn't pay for this kind of long term nonsense, so those people were targeted based on the nature of insurance that they had. Every year Psychiatry industry defrauds the government and private insurance of 40 billion dollars using any means possible.

Dr. Gary Null said, "There were some advertisements very seductive advertisements for people who want to lose weight and were having a problem with losing weight. They had this all-expense paid spa and when they went to that spa, it wasn't a spa. It was a Psychiatric center and then they couldn't get out."

Dennis Cowan health care fraud consultant said, "Those people received massive doses of mind altering drugs and they were kept there for a lengthy period of time and their insurance provider was billed tremendous amount of money for something that was unnecessary."

Beyond greed and deceit, psychiatrists from time to time have been caught for sex crimes.

This has happened despite the high probability of getting away with such crimes. Why? Who believes a mentally ill female or a kid? And the treatment with very private and things often don't leak out. Their sex crimes often involved children.

Dr. Charles Markham Berry, a prominent Atlanta psychiatrist known for his Christian counselling and volunteer work at local orphanages, was sentenced to 20 years in prison on federal and state charges of child molestation and child pornography. He sexually abused children of age 7 to 17.

This is not an isolated incident in the Psychiatric profession. In every country, you will find psychiatrist committing rape, crimes, murder, and frauds.

You cannot exercise power or influence without credibility so psychiatry manufacturer its own. Hence came the Diagnostic and statistical manual (DSM) of mental disorders. We will look into the history of the DSM in the next chapter.

The American Psychiatric Association is the one which publishes the DSM. Any hypothesis needs a scientific foundation to be accepted by the general public.

But here is the problem. The committee of psychiatrist meets once in a while to decide upon the mental disorders. They simply **VOTE** if a particular human condition can be called a mental disorder. All in favour say "Aye". That is it. It all started with DSM-I with 100 mental disorders. Now after 60 years later the present DSM-5 has over 374 mental disorders. Can you believe it?

And there is no laboratory test available to confirm if a person is actually having any of the 374 conditions defined in the DSM. There is no test to identify if someone has improved after the administration of drugs. DSM contains a bunch of definitions and questionnaires which more like a qualitative symptoms and person might be asked to answer 10 or more questions by a Psychiatrist and simply labelled patient for life. No lab test or scan is required. All we need is a DSM manual and a psychiatrist to make you a mentally ill. Simple!

Neil Willner works in an insurance firm said, "If you have 27 mental disorders in DSM, which is 27 ways to bill. If you have 300 ways in DSM, that is 300 ways to bill. You can find pretty much anyone walking on the streets to fit into a DSM."

An arithmetic learning disorder is an official Psychiatric diagnosis. General anxiety disorder is an official Psychiatric diagnosis. Reading disorder is an official Psychiatric diagnosis. Do you think there can be a pill to make someone smart in mathematics? Well, psychiatrists believe they can!

Many hidden camera tests have been carried up by sane people to prove that Psychiatry is completely bogus. There is no way to know if someone is sane or not. In one such experiment, a person went to 7 different psychiatrists and told them the same symptoms. All the 7 came up with a different diagnosis which ranged from ADD to ADHD to bipolar to brain chemistry disorder to depression.

Many Psychiatrists have come on camera and admitted that they don't know what causes mental disorders. When you don't know what causes it, how do you plan to treat it?

Wherever you find a Psychiatric diagnosis you will find a corresponding Psychiatric drug. This is an unholy Nexus and you shouldn't be surprised to know that almost 60% of the DSM committee members have direct financial ties to one or more pharmaceutical company. Pharma fund the researches of professors and indirectly train the whole medical education on the use of drugs for all symptoms. Most Psychiatrists don't spend a minute to understand why a patient is distressed. Their only job is to find a diagnosis and a subsequent laundry list of drugs.

Symptoms that fail to meet the diagnostic criteria for a recognized mental disorder may fall under the broad category of "other mental disorders." The DSM-5 recognizes four disorders in this category:

- Other specified mental disorder due to a medical condition

- Unspecified mental disorder due to a medical condition

- Other specified mental disorder

- Unspecified mental disorder

The catch-all category of "unspecified mental disorder" also drew criticism from some psychiatrists and psychologists for what they feel are a lack of precision. The only criterion for receiving the diagnosis is that the patient does not "meet the full criteria for any mental disorder." This, they suggest, might mean that people fail to receive a correct and more specific diagnosis which might ultimately lead to them not receiving the right treatment for their condition. What this also means is that no one who enters a psychiatrist's office should go without chemical prescriptions.

Psychiatrists have labelled 450 million people worldwide based on the DSM. If you are to believe the DSM, each and every person on this planet can be labelled as mentally ill. Pharma would not even spare animals and label them as mentally ill, in future.

A few decades back, psychiatrists decided to target the American school system; *find them when they are young.* By 1960s psychiatry little by little entered the US schools. By 1965, it was written into law - Psychiatry was given freedom to wholesale labelling and drugging of school children. The Act to drug children was called *Educational Act of 1965 elementary and secondary education.*

"A child is labelled ADD or ADHD the minute he cannot sit still for 10 min or he talks constantly or ignores the teacher completely. That would get him or her into ADD or ADHD label. The labelling of ADHD in the US went in full swing in 1987. Within 1 year 500,000 American children were diagnosed as ADHD. By 1994, that number has increased to 4.5 million," said Beverly Eakman

2 years later the number of American students labelled as ADHD reached a shocking 6 million. Today 20 million children worldwide are labelled with some form of mental disorder diagnosis of which is often made in a matter of 5 minutes. During the same period, the sales of Psychiatric drugs to children skyrocketed to 32 times.

Children are not asking to be diagnosed. Children are not complaining. They don't want to be called crazy. As Doctor Thomas said, "Ask the classic Roman question: who benefits?" It's the people who make the diagnosis.

Remember those school firings in the US. There is now enough proof that many of those students were taking those psychiatric pills.

A founding father of ADHD announced a few months before his death that 'ADHD is a prime example of a fictitious disease'. After turning 87 years old, American psychiatrist Dr. Leon Eisenberg made this statement to the German weekly Der Spiegel and seven months later, he died. Apparently, he had decided to clean his conscience before moving to the beyond. Dr. Edward C. Hamlyn, a founding member of the Royal College of General Practitioners, in 1998 stated, "ADHD is fraud intended to justify starting children on a life of drug addiction."

Psychiatry revealed their master plan in 1960s. G. Brock was the co-founder of world federation for mental health. He revealed the Psychiatric plan, "to achieve world government it is necessary to remove from the minds of men their individualism, loyalty to family traditions, national patriotism and religious dogmas."

Osama bin laden was characterised as the mastermind behind 9/11. But the real man behind the attack was his trusted partner - Ayman Al-Zawahiri. He was educated in psychology and pharmacology at the University of Cairo. He was also the author of the Al Qaeda training manual on the use of coercive Psychiatry.

Prof. Barry Mehler said, "When you look at Psychiatry and psychology, social control is the primary agenda." Psychiatry is always about politics and they have an agenda to rule your brains. The idea is to use force against the people who don't want force.

Psychiatrist Dr. Heinz Lehman said, "Psychiatry should actually go into government and politicians should listen to psychiatrists. Politicians should listen to psychiatrists and (psychiatry) should direct and monitor political activities."

Psychiatry is now planning to mass screen all the 55 million children in the US with a 10 min questionnaire. Not even that, their plan is to also include the parents and slowly the entire population.

Psychiatry is arguably the least science-based of all the medical specialties, and Freudian psychoanalysis is arguably the least science-based psychotherapy. A new book, *Freud: The Making of an Illusion*, by Frederick Crews, has explained how Freud's theories were completely false and made up. Freud's theories have been widely criticized as unscientific, and treatment of mental disorders has increasingly turned to psychotropic medications and effective therapies like cognitive behavioural therapy (CBT). Freud's impact on 20th century thought is undeniable, but he got almost everything wrong.

I can go on and on but i believe you have got the gist. History of psychiatry is such that no psychiatrist can be proud of it. There is no science of mentally ill here. I don't the new age psychiatrists as well as they are simply doing what they were taught in their medical colleges. Patients are tortured, labelled with disorders to milk money. Yes, there may be people who need help but giving them dangerous chemicals for life is not a solution. Also the belief that billions, who are suffering some sort of symptoms of mental illness including stress and anxiety, have brain or genetic disorders in completely flawed. Drugging people by keeping the premise of DSM and chemical imbalance needs to stop.

Shubham Gupta

3. Psychiatry's bible - DSM

Life throws challenges to all of us. Life can be full of adventure – hot, fast slow, and sad; sometimes even filled with ups and downs. People's emotional problems are real. Anxiety, sadness, depression are human reactions to life challenges. We all react differently to different situations. We are not machines that will react the same way when our buttons are pushed. Sometimes, even the machines do not behave the same.

Based on how a child is raised, he or she can develop certain behaviours and patterns. Someone might easily get tensed while others are able to sail through tough situations. Someone might completely breakdown at the death of a loved one while others might take the event in its true essence. Sometimes when we are not able to take the situation on our own, we seek help. Nobody who is emotionally and physically strong will ever walk to a doctor. But according to psychiatry, any part of life can be labelled as a mental illness.

If you are sad after a bad breakup or a divorce; you can be labelled as depressed. If you are nervous speaking in public, you can be diagnosed with Social anxiety disorder. If you are talkative or super active, you can be labelled as a manic. If you are having ups and downs, you can be diagnosed as Bipolar. If you suspect others, you can be labelled as Paranoid Personality disorder. If you have homesickness, you can be labelled with Separation anxiety disorder. If you are addicted to internet gaming, you can be diagnosed with Internet Gaming Disorder. If you love to binge eat, you can be diagnosed with Binge Eating Disorder. If you are trying to leave caffeine and having a tough time, you can be diagnosed with Caffeine Withdrawal Disorder. If your child is friendly with strangers, he or she can be diagnosed with Disinhibited Social

Engagement Disorder. If you have persistent difficulty discarding or parting with possessions, you can be labelled to have Hoarding Disorder.

This might sound crazy but that is how psychiatry labels all personalities and lifestyles. Psychiatrists have successfully convinced the public that all the common life situations and personalities are brain diseases. This has to be the greatest and the most successful marketing campaign ever in history. Psychiatry is an industry built on beliefs and marketing and making more than 350 billion dollars a year.

From where do the psychiatrists get their knowledge and diagnosis? It's the DSM. DSM stands for Diagnostic and Statistical Manual of Mental Disorders. There is almost no statistical analysis in this 943 pages manual. It covers over 370 illness including mathematics disorder, fear of spiders, nightmares. Psychiatry and DSM have taken basic life problems and challenges and reinterpreted them as brain diseases.

When such was the theory, you would expect a lot of backing of science and technology but turns out that there is no scientific basis for any of the conditions mentioned in the DSM. In fact, the DSM committee's psychiatrists have admitted that they meet once in a while and vote to make human behaviour as a mental illness. The chairman would bring out a name and if there are enough shows of hands in favour, then congratulations - you have a new mental illness. Since there are no biological tests available for psychiatry, diagnosis for any mental illness described in the DSM is based on checklists and questionnaires.

The diagnosis is highly subjective and often dependent upon the psychiatrist in front of the patient. This has been proven time and again.

DSM started with a desire to make psychiatry and psychology to be accepted by mainstream medicine. Before the DSM era, psychiatrists occupied the lowest rug of the medical profession. They work almost exclusively in a mental asylum as caretakers for the mentally ill. They had no cures for anything and people had very little regard for them as "real" doctors.

There was no science backing psychiatry. There was little chance for them to be ever respected by the public and their peers as real doctors.

Psychiatrist Dr. Ron Leifer said, "Psychiatrists wanted to be viewed as physicians and doctors and in order to be viewed as doctors, the people they dealt with have to be viewed as patients. And if doctors dealt with diseases, then their patients have to be diseased."

Psychiatrists found this wonderful opportunity to become respected in the eyes of their peers. "We psychologist have always desperately wanted to be accepted as a real science as true science. Now what the early psychologist and psychiatrists did was that they looked around and saw what other scientists were doing and they decided to emulate them," admitted psychologist Dr. Louis Wynne.

In the 1950s psychiatry and psychology came up with DSM-I, an official book on the so-called "mental diseases" cataloguing 112 mental disorders. Mental disorders were invented and voted into the DSM-I by a bunch of Psychiatrists. This book catalogued normal human behaviours as mental illnesses including breath holding, nail biting, thumb sucking, somnambulism, poor efficiency, and even homosexuality. By defining more and more life as abnormal, psychiatry was aiming legitimacy, respect and also to get a huge amount of government money.

The next version of DSM-II came in 1968 which expanded the mental diseases from 112 to 176 again to grab even more insurance and government money. To do this internationally, the DSM-II was specifically written in mind with the International classification of diseases (ICD), a book used extensively across Europe and around the world. DSM was made larger and larger with no backing of science and statistics. There is no lab research behind those names or disorders being voted in the DSM. It's just random words being tossed around which can label human behaviours as mentally illness.

Meanwhile, the diseases in DSM-III ballooned to 269. Homosexuality which was listed in the DSM - I and II as mental disease, was finally voted out in DSM-III. Do you think there was a science behind such a change in the stance? No. Homosexuality was kept in the DSM for political and religious reasons and removed for political reasons. Do you think this is anywhere near to science?

Psychiatrists were still not getting accepted as real doctors. The diagnosis was not scientific and they were not able to treat anyone.

To make the diagnosis sound more scientific, the psychiatrists had to coin more scientific-sounding terms. Hence, they invented the word - chemical imbalance. This theory suggested why depression might be caused - an imbalance of certain brain chemicals called neurotransmitters. Professor of Psychiatry Dr. Joseph Schildkraut hypothesized that because psychiatric drugs altered some of these brain chemicals than mental illnesses must be caused by too much or too little of it. It is like saying because aspirin stops the headaches, headaches are caused by the deficiency of aspirin.

However absurd, this theory was able to give a much needed artificial aura of science to psychiatry. Psychiatry got the much-needed elixir. Since then, the word "Chemical Imbalance" has been tossed around by psychiatry. Funny thing, nobody has ever proven this theory of chemical imbalance but it has been so often repeated that soon people forgot that it was a hypothesis and not a conclusion. Psychiatry went even further. They even linked this chemical imbalance to our genes. Why? So that now psychiatry can hide their incapability of curing anyone behind the gene theory. Now they can blame your genes for your problem and move from curing to "managing" your condition.

The pharmaceutical industry and psychiatry have heavily promoted this chemical Imbalance theory. "You come to my office and I say to you - well you describe what's going on in your life and I say well it's clear to me that you got a chemical imbalance and I am going to write you a prescription for this. The truth of the matter is there is no such thing as a chemical Imbalance," said psychologist Louis Wynne. There is no test out there on which Psychiatry and psychology can depend upon to prove the chemical imbalance theory.

The Psychiatry will try to explain to you that you have depression because you have less serotonin or dopamine (neurotransmitters) and this medicine will balance the imbalance. Serotonin is a chemical and neurotransmitter in the human body. It is believed to help regulate mood and social behaviour, appetite and digestion, sleep, memory, and sexual desire and function. "We have already proven that there is nothing wrong with the serotonin levels. It is completely a myth," said Psychiatrist Dr. Colin Ross.

Psychiatric diagnosis is made purely based on personal opinion. BBC even did a documentary on this. They invited 10 volunteers - 5 considered normal, 5 previously diagnosed as mentally ill and 3 well known mental health experts. The 3 experts were supposed to observe the volunteers and determine who was who.

After whole 1 week of observation, they only identified 2 out 5 disorders. So much for Science!!

From time and time again the DSM committee has admitted that they cannot define mental disorder. It is mentioned in the DSM-IV that: Although this manual provides a classification of mental disorders, it must be admitted that no definition adequately specifies precise boundaries for the concept of mental disorder.

DSM - IV had 374 mental disorders catalogued. In just 40 years, the psychiatry moved from 112 to 374 diseases. In order to diagnose a person with any mental illness, those disorders must be added in the DSM. With the help of the DSM, 120 million people have been diagnosed with some form of mental diagnosis.

Psychiatry doesn't want to understand WHY of any conditions mentioned in the DSM. Most patients admit that within 15 minutes of entering a room with a psychiatrist, they walk away with prescription medicine. 98% of the patients walk away with medication. That's how pharmacology has integrated well with the DSM. A Psychiatrist, who tells the patient that they don't have any mental problem, will not have a busy practice. DSM has actually become an official manual to prescribe pharmaceutical drugs.

Over 600 million Psychiatric prescriptions are written in a year! In case a patient refuses to take prescribed medication, DSM has a disorder for that too. Noncompliance with treatment is a way to trap people who refuse to take medicine. This means that you are mentally ill if you don't do what a Psychiatrist tells you to do! A Psychiatrist has 370 options to choose from. He will label you with one or the other diagnosis.

Psycho-pharma lobby has been effective in laws being passed forcing insurance companies to provide mental health insurance comparable to regular medical insurance. The pharma now bills around $72 billion from private insurance.

With new disorders being introduced, the current version of DSM-5 has been in the market since 2013. Despite heavy criticism, the American Psychiatric Association (APA) continues to promote and support the DSM committee. There has been proof now that more than 56% of the psychiatrists on the DSM committee panel have financial ties with one or more pharmaceutical companies. There is a huge conflict of interest and DSM has now become a puppet in the hands of the pharma industry.

One of the more controversial changes was to eliminate the previous DSM's "bereavement exclusion" for depression. Now, if a father grieves for a murdered or dead child for more than a couple of weeks, he is mentally ill. A footnote in the DSM-5 explains that "the inability to anticipate happiness or pleasure" in such a situation is a diagnostic criterion for the mental disorder of depression.

To some, this smacks of pathologizing a normal, understandable human reaction. "This completely leaves the person out of the equation and turns people into patients," said psychotherapist Eric Maisel, a critic of the DSM. "The DSM claims that an unwanted, distressing feeling is a sign of a disorder rather than being just a feeling, and it isn't at all interested in whether your circumstances could have caused those feelings."

It is important to consider circumstances, he said, because if someone experiences deep anxiety as a result of losing her job, becoming ill or facing foreclosure, "the remedy shouldn't be a pill," the usual outcome of a diagnosis of "generalized anxiety disorder."

4. Cheating the drug approval process

You might be wondering if these psychotropic drugs don't work on the public at large, why there are so many of them approved in the last few decades.

Since psychotropic drugs are made up of dangerous compounds, they are tightly regulated by governments throughout the world. For any new psychotropic drug to get approval for use, it must undergo tests intended to protect the public. When a pharmaceutical company wants to send a drug for approval, it has to test the drug through multiple rounds of clinical trials. They have to provide safety data to the government agencies that this is a safe and effective drug to treat a human condition.

In clinical trials, pharma engages psychiatrists to do the research and here lies the first weak spot of the drug testing process. We can bank on the fact that these reputed psychiatrists have some or the other financial ties with the very pharmaceutical company for which they are testing the drug. This is the step where the system starts to get rigged. A trail which should be completely unbiased does not remain to be so. This is a terrible terrible thing in the drug approval process.

"The desperate thing about this is that it is all dressed up in the name of science. It is not science. It's pure marketing. They get away with it because it is called science," said author Barry Hubbard. The biggest problem is that there is no science of biochemical imbalance. On top of that, psychiatrists are willing to test these dangerous drugs on human beings.

The clinical trials are supposed to be conducted in four phases of which the results of the first three phases must be submitted to the government body for regulatory approvals.

1.   Phase I: In phase I, the drug is tested for toxicity and tolerability. If the drug clears this hurdle then it moves to the next phase.

2.   Phase II: In phase II, the drug is tested for its effectiveness; how it interacts with the body.

3.   Phase III: In phase III, the drug is compared with a placebo and tested if it is actually better than a sugar pill or not.

4.   Phase IV: In phase IV, the drug companies are expected to conduct 'post-approval' studies. Companies are supposed to watch out for actual effects of the drug on the general public. It is this phase where the whole public becomes the lab rats for the pharma drug testing. When the drug hits the ethnic groups, then we see how many suicides are happening, how many heart attacks are happening, how many are having seizures.

With no scientific or laboratory tests, psychiatric drug testing remains extremely subjective. They cannot measure your condition before and after administering a drug. It all comes down to questionnaires and individual assessment. With big money at stake, psychiatric drug testing can easily be manipulated. Dr. Howard Brody of the University of Texas said, "There are many many places where you can tweak the study just a little bit with the study design or the way you gather data or the way data is reported."

Many from the same profession have confirmed the level of manipulation that happens in reporting the data. One of the common manipulations goes like this:

Suppose you start a clinical trial with 100 people - 40% drop out during the studies. 30% have a positive response while 30% has no response. They then say that they have a 50% response rate. Most of us would say it is only a 30% response rate because only 30 out of actual 100 responded. But the researchers and pharma get away with such fudging of data. They would even completely ignore the side-effects that the 40% had because which they dropped out from the studies. One more trick exhibited here is that in case anyone has a negative effect during the trail, the person is marked as "dropout" so that they don't have to report the data. The psychiatrists involved in collecting the data also manipulate/change the data reported by the subjects.

That is only the tip of the iceberg in terms of data manipulations that can be done.

One more thing that you must have noticed is that the drug companies completely own testing their own drugs. It's like giving the thief the key to the lockers and asks him to guard the money. He will get tempted to open the locker and take some money. History is filled with hundreds of drugs which were once approved by the government agencies were banned years later.

Cylert which was a medication for ADHD/ADD was recalled from the market after 30 years as it causes liver toxicity. Accutane was removed from the market after 27 years as it increased the risk of birth defects, miscarriages, and premature births when used by pregnant women; inflammatory bowel disease; suicidal tendencies. Recently Indian government agency banned 344 drugs from the market as they found them non-efficacies.

These are just a few examples of how the drug approval process has been rigged from many decades. If you want to know more about the banned drugs visit the websites of the regulatory bodies of those countries. Remember that all these drugs were once actually found to be effective and safe for human consumption and treatment of a disease in the clinical trials.

When drug companies are entrusted testing their own drugs, public will continue to become the guinea pigs for phase IV testing phase. Pharma will focus on the things they want to see and continue to report only those. They would ignore all the trial results which don't help in getting the approval for their magic pills. Drug companies can very easily under-report the side-effects and over exaggerate the positive effects for patients. The similar trend was found in the lipid theory. The whole cholesterol myth was created by fudging the data by a physiologist called Ancel Keys. In particular, he hypothesized that dietary saturated fat causes cardiovascular heart disease and should be avoided. We all saw what happened post that. Now people are slowly realizing the harmful effects of not eating saturated fats.I believe that statistics as science is designed to fool. Probably that is why it is used to so heavily in scientific studies.

Another classic example of fraud can be spotted in clinical trials for an SNRI antidepressant approved in 2004 by FDA. In that clinical trial, healthy normal people were included who had no symptoms of clinical depression. Sach Oliver who was the trial attorney said, "In that clinical trial there were 11 attempted suicides and 4 suicides completed. One of which was Tracy Johnson a 19-year-old college girl. She didn't have any symptoms of depression and yet this drug pushed her to suicide by hanging herself."

The above case should be a glaring rebuttal to people who claim that people commit suicides because of an underlying illness. These drugs have the capability to push healthy or mildly depressed people to end their lives sometimes even to kill others. They don't want to live anymore. Despite the controversy, the FDA went ahead and approved the drug based on the clinical research data.

Since pharma is in a rush to make more money, most clinical trials happen for a very short period of time. Most trials are completed in 4 to 8 weeks. That is it! It is outrageous that a billion dollar industry is spending so less time in testing the effects of their own drugs over a period of time. Even if the researcher decides to report the correct data, in 5 weeks you might definitely not see any major side effects. Public, on the other hand, is supposed to consume these drug for their lifetime.

One consumer protection group has advised patients to refuse any drug which has not been in the market for at least 7 years. It is only after 7 years of a drug in marketing that we really see the efficacy of the drug. Imagine! If you are taking a drug which has been on the market for a year or two, you are acting as a guinea pig for the pharma.

Children are our future but according to psychiatry children are mentally ill. FDA did something really wonderful in 2001. To encourage pharma to test drugs for children, they gave an incentive which was later passed in the parliament. They now give 6-month additional patent period to pharma who have also tested their drugs for their efficacies for children. This 6-month exclusivity generally amounts to more than a billion dollars of sales. Savvy!

With this kind of money at stake, children are now rampantly involved in the testing of these dangerous drugs. These drugs which are only a few percentage points better than placebo comes with a laundry list of side-effects. Parents and children are told that these drugs are safe for consumption.

FDA panels that evaluate these drugs are largely psychiatrists. These psychiatrists generally have financial ties with many pharmaceutical companies. An FDA panellist can also be an industry speaker or a paid speaker to a pharma convention or can be on a pharma board.

Once a drug gets its approval from the approval agency, the next step is now purely marketing. The next step is to convince the local psychiatrists to start prescribing the drugs to the patients. In this exercise, pharma spends more money than it actually spends on researching for the revolutionary drug. Pharma hires the so-called renowned experts and PR firms to spread the word. There are a lot of academic psychiatrists who have ties to multiple companies who make a large amount of money in this game. The role of this person is to feed all his peers about this new miracle drug.

The medical schools need funding to do research. Pharma is quick to grant awards. Now drug companies are building research centres right next to the medical colleges. University of Michigan depression center received 750,000 dollars of a grant from Eli Lilly foundation in 2002. With research being completely hacked and dependent on pharma money, you can understand that the results of those studies will be to benefit the pharmaceutical that is funding those researches. There is no free lunch in this world.

Pharma money has completely corrupted the institutional research credibility. Even Harvard University is no better. Harvard recently earned an 'F' from the American Medical Student Association, which grades medical schools' conflict-of-interest policies on money from the pharmaceutical industry. ProPublica reported - "Harvard also faced embarrassment when Sen. Charles Grassley (R-IA) accused two of its psychiatrists of potentially breaking federal and university conflict-of-interest rules by failing to fully report huge fees from drug companies."

Not only this, pharma has also successfully invaded in school curriculums to make sure the new psychiatrist who pass out from these colleges only prescribe drugs to treat different symptoms. A Psychiatrist is now trained for only one purpose - to prescribe psychiatric drugs.

Another PR activity is to push out a lot of ghost articles with researches about the efficacies of the new drugs in treating certain symptoms. Almost 50% of such research is ghost-written, where a paid psychiatrist name (as if he was the author) is then put on to the article and published in renowned journals. These journals are read by peers who get influenced by these supposedly unbiased reports. These journals are often sent free to psychiatrists and doctors under the guise of legitimate medical research. Why are they free? Because pharma is ready to buy most of the pages of the magazine for advertisements. It's a marketing tool for the pharma.

You can realize the conflict of interest. Journals have turned into marketing avenues for pharmaceuticals. Journals will never dare to report a negative article against a pharma company that buys advertisements in the journal.

Apart from this, the medical representatives reward the psychiatrists who are the star prescribers of their drugs. From expensive lunches, dinners, free game passes to an exotic holiday destination in the guise of conferences where there will be speakers paid by the very pharma company, are rewarded to the psychiatrists.

You can now understand that there is no science involved in rolling out new drugs. It is all pure and simple marketing. The better the marketing, the more the sales.

51

5. Drugging the entire world

The pharmaceutical industry is the world's third biggest industry minting over 1.5 trillion dollars a year. The number 1 and 2 are Arms & ammunition and tobacco & alcohol industries respectively. How did pharma become so big in such a quick time? With so much scientific and technological advances, we would expect a healthier world. We would expect a world where fewer people would fall ill. Is it not so? While the industry boast that the life expectancy has been increased from nobody knows what numbers, but are we really healthier than our past generations? We cannot be, right? Else how will you explain the increasing revenue of the pharma companies?

In the renowned book Selling Sickness, author Ray Moynihan recount the candid comments made by the retiring CEO of Merck. "Thirty years ago…Merck's aggressive chief executive Henry Gadsden told Fortune magazine of his distress that the company's potential markets had been limited to sick people. Suggesting he'd rather have Merck to be more like chewing gum maker Wrigley, Gadsden said it had long been his dream to make drugs for healthy people. Because then, Merck would be able to sell to everyone." Three decades on, the late Henry Gadsden's dream has come true."

Mental illness is a serious business for pharma. Almost 1/3rd of all the revenue which is close to $ 350 billion come from selling psychotropic drugs. That is huge money and pharma has taken its business very seriously. Now let's look at the business model of pharmaceuticals. Although they promote their brands as all out for health and well being, there is a huge conflict of self-interest. Why? Like any industry, for pharma, the main goal is money and profits. For their CEO, the main goal is increasing the shareholder's value. Is it not? Now there are three big problems here:

1. Curing a patient would be a very bad business model. If you cure people, you are losing business, isn't it? Thinking of pharma as a

business is serious error. It cannot be allowed to run as a profit making machine. That is why world is in such a mess.

2.   Where in the business model, does the health of the patient come? Nowhere! The main aim is to get as many prescriptions as possible from the doctors to the general public. If the people stop falling ill, pharma is in big trouble.

3. More the number of non-curable diseases, better opportunity to sell more drugs. That is why we have hardly see any cure for any diseases but we see more and more blockbuster pills to "manage" our illness. There can be two reasons for such a scenario. Either, we don't understand why something is happening or we don't want to find a cure for it at all.

Psychotropic medicines are available only on prescription and you are not the one who decides which medicine. The patient never chooses what medicine to take. Doctors do that for you. Doctors are the consumers of pharma products but they are not the ones consuming it. Ironic! Now, doctors rarely know what a drug will do to the patient. They have to trust the Pharma Company and the company's medical representatives to provide the correct information. In this whole model, the goal is to push the maximum prescription of a drug in a month. Health is nowhere in the picture. If you heal fine, if not, then take another higher dose pill.

Do you see the conflict of interest? That is the main reason why pharma and researchers have not found out cure to any disease in the last many decades. They have found ways to "manage" most of the disease. Why? Because that's like having a customer for lifetime. That is the best business model for them. If they start healing cancer or diabetes, then where is the shareholder's value in that? That is a BAD business model.

Now let's come to the psychotropic drugs. From the last few chapters, you must have already understood the bad history of psychiatry and how it runs purely on propaganda and marketing. Pharma is in bed with psychiatry for no other reason than it is the best business model for both of them. You can make anybody sick based on the clues from DSM and drug them for life.

For treating mental illnesses ranging from depression to bipolar, pharma has come up with hundreds of pharmaceutical drugs. Antidepressants are the most prescribed drugs. Funny thing is that the exact mechanism of how antidepressants work in unknown. The prevailing theory is that antidepressants increase the concentration of one or more brain chemicals (neurotransmitters) that nerves in the brain use to communicate with one another. The neurotransmitters affected by antidepressants are norepinephrine, serotonin, and dopamine.

Let's look at the most common drugs categories which are administered to people.

1.   SSRIs: Selective serotonin reuptake inhibitors (SSRIs) are the latest and the most widely used type of antidepressants. SSRIs are also prescribed for conditions like OCD, GAD, phobias, PTSD and many others.

How SSRIs work? Nobody really knows how these drugs work but the belief is that these drugs work by increasing the happy hormone - serotonin in the brain. The more the happy hormone is there in your brain, the more happy you will be. That is the logic behind this drug. Even a layman can understand that this is a misinterpreted causality. A drug has no intelligence of its own. It is simply a bunch of chemicals which are released into our bloodstream. These chemicals will hit each and every cell of your body and not just a particular brain cell. The belief that the chemicals increase serotonin in a specific place in the brain has to be completely made up.

According to the NHS website, SSRIs are "usually the first choice medication for depression" because they "generally have fewer side effects".

"These can be troublesome at first, but they'll generally improve with time," it says.

It says the "common side effects" of the drugs can include: "Feeling agitated, shaky or anxious; feeling or being sick; dizziness; blurred vision; low sex drive; difficulty achieving orgasm during sex or masturbation; in men, difficulty obtaining or maintaining an erection."

This is exactly what i am trying to explain. Mind you, these are just a very short list of side-effects of SSRIs. Actual side-effects range in thousands. Pharma knows that these drugs don't work but there are billions of dollars at stake. They will continue their propaganda that mental illness is a big problem and their drugs are needed to treat the people.

Testimony presented by experts at the first day of hearings held by the US Food and Drug Administration confirmed that depressed children who are treated with antidepressants are more likely to harm themselves than depressed children treated with placebo. These are some of the testimonies of the parents and people describing their experiences with antidepressants in front of the FDA panel:

"I went from being a shy and mildly depressed but never suicidal kid to being overcome with the thoughts of hurting and killing myself while on the SSRIs drugs; thoughts on which i acted on."

"He told me that i cannot stand the way this drug makes me feel. Two days later he committed suicide."

"She died on suicide at age 12 years and 3 months, just eight weeks after being put on Paxil and then Zoloft."

Dr. Mark Hudak who was part of the FDA committee meeting admitted, "Lot of the people who spoke this morning, the picture that was presented of their child was someone who was not someone who was very ill or someone who had relatively minor type of findings were put on these drugs which had terrible consequences."

After reports of increased cases of suicide, in 2004, the Food and Drug Administration (FDA) issued a black-box warning on antidepressants indicating that they were associated with an increased risk of suicidal thinking, feeling, and behaviour in young people. Can you believe it? A medicine which can actually give you suicidal thoughts!

Why would a drug which is supposed to relieve people of depression is expected to make them anxious, suicidal? A new study published in the journal Nature has found that contrary to popular belief that serotonin only promotes happy feelings; it also has a darker side. Researchers delivered a mild shock to the paws of mice and found this activated neurons that produce serotonin in an area of the brain known to be involved in mood and depression.

Artificially increasing these neurons' activity also appeared to make the mice anxious. Using sophisticated equipment to monitor the mice's brains, the scientists, from North Carolina University's medical school, then mapped what they described as an "essential" serotonin-driven circuit "governing fear and anxiety".

Biochemically, serotonin is primarily found (almost 90%) in gastrointestinal tract, which regulates intestinal movement. Serotonin regulates numerous biological processes including cardiovascular function, bowel motility, ejaculatory latency, and bladder control. Nobody completely understands what all functions this hormone is taking care of. Yet, pharma is meddling with this hormone in the body when 90% of which is actually found in our gut. Despite all that, this hormone is called the happiness hormone. How stupid can we really be?

Now let's see how psychiatry defines serotonin.

"Serotonin is a neurotransmitter that is synthesized, stored, and released by specific neurons in the brain. Natural Serotonin is involved in the regulation of several processes within the brain, including, depression, mood, emotions, aggression, sleep, appetite, anxiety, memory, and perceptions. Serotonin regulates these processes through pathways that innervate (connect to) different brain regions. Most cells in the brain, over 40 million, are either directly or indirectly affected by serotonin levels as well as muscles, and parts of the cardiovascular and endocrine systems. Because of this far reaching influence, low serotonin levels are often attributed to anxiety, panic attacks, obesity, insomnia, and fibromyalgia." - Integrative psychiatry (website)

They have completely ignored the fact that serotonin is mostly present in the gut and is involved for so many other things than promoting happiness.

A hormone, which is involved in so many areas of a normal human body, is dangerously meddled with. We are messing with a normal working human body in the name of treatment of a condition which is not even a disease. No wonder, so many people who are on these drugs or trying to leave these drugs commit homicides and suicides. The medicine is literally designed to make you sick. I don't want to talk about MAOIs and TCAs class of antidepressants. Why? Because SSRIs are considered the most efficient of the bunch with least side effects.

Withdrawal from any antidepressant medications can cause severe psychiatric and/or physical problems. Withdrawal can cause a wide range of symptoms, from headaches, brain "zaps", insomnia, lethargy or fatigue, to feeling anger, irritation or even extreme, uncontrollable rage, and countless others. It might take up to 1 year or more to come out safely from these drugs. It is almost like being on actual drugs like heroin or cocaine. Patients have also reported that it is easier to come out of cocaine addiction then from these psychotropic drugs. Why will a medicine cause such a withdrawal symptom? It's good for the pharma! Patients will demand from the doctors these drugs as withdrawing from them is really difficult.

Isn't this a slight hint that these drugs are not helping the patients but are actually making them addicted to those chemicals?

There have been 135,587 Adverse Drug Reactions in connection with antidepressants that have been reported to the FDA's Adverse Event Reporting System (MedWatch), between 2004 and 2012. For those of you who don't know, ADR was once found to be the biggest killer of the people of America, even above cancer and heart attacks.

The FDA estimates that less than 1% of all serious events are ever reported to it, so the actual number of side effects occurring is most certainly higher.

- 10,707 cases of drug withdrawal syndrome

- 10,210 cases of nausea

- 9,508 cases of dizziness

- 9,399 cases of the drug being ineffective

- 8,376 cases of anxiety

- 7,774 cases of headache

- 7,750 cases of insomnia

- 7,659 cases of depression

- 6,814 cases of suicidal Ideation

- 6,134 cases of fatigue

There is now enough proof that the SSRIs actually cause depression and anxiety. They are not designed to help your depression but to make you mentally ill so that you can be a lifetime customer of pharma. Biggest controversy became evident when usage of SSRIs was found to be directly correlated to mass school shooting in the US. These people had no history of violence suddenly after put on these SSRI drugs started killing people they didn't even know.

You might remember the October 2017 shooting in Las Vegas. At least 59 people have been killed and another 527 injured in a mass shooting at a Las Vegas concert. FBI investigated the case but closed it when it didn't find any motivation or intention. Even the brother of Stephen Paddock, the Las Vegas shooter, was shocked to hear his brother's name as the shooter of the incidence. The Las Vegas Review-Journal reported that Paddock was prescribed the anti-anxiety drug diazepam, better known by its brand name, Valium, in June that year. Why will a 64-years old man, with no intention, murder so many people? Well, FBI couldn't answer that. Is this just a coincidence?

15-year-old Kip Kinkel was withdrawing from Prozac when he shot 22 school classmates, killing two of them after killing his parents at home. Coincidence?

Jason Hoffman opened fire at Granite Hills High School, injuring three students and two teachers in El Cajon, California, a suburb of San Diego. Hoffman, 18-years-old at the time of the rampage, had been diagnosed as being clinically depressed and was taking the antidepressants prior to the shooting. Hoffman's mother said her son had an adverse reaction to his antidepressant medication. The teen was facing 27 years to life in prison when officials discovered that he had hung himself in his jail cell. Coincidence?

Matthew Skalitzky stabbed and beheaded his 68-year-old mother, Jane Skalitzky, with a 4-foot sword shortly after having breakfast with his parents at their home in Sun Prairie, Wisconsin on September 16, 2015, according to Madison.com. Matthew Skalitzky was diagnosed with mental illness and had reportedly stopped taking his prescribed medication after reading "negative comments" about the drugs online, but resumed taking them a few days before the attack, according to Matthew Skalitzky's father. Coincidence?

17-year-old TJ Solomon was on a mix of antidepressants when he aimed a shotgun at his classmates killing 6. Coincidence?

17-year-old Eric Harris was on psychotropic drugs when he killed 12 classmates and a teacher. In many of the barbaric shootings, one or more psychotropic drug was always in picture although hidden from most. Coincidence?

There are hundreds of such shooting or killing cases, where the person with no violent history, resorted to killing people in extreme rage. Pharma and psychiatrists will continue to deny the causation but we have to understand that they will. They will not easily admit that their medicines are not only useless but fatal in treating any human mental conditions.

Psychiatrist Dr. Peter Breggin said, "One of the things that we have known in the past about depression is it that it very very rarely leads to violence. It's only since the advent of these new SSRI drugs that we have murderers sometimes even mass murderers taking anti-depressant drugs."

Dr. David Healy said, "What is happening is that we are not just picking up people who were ill and need to be treated, we have gone way way beyond that by actually making people ill."

Psychiatrists and government are quick to dismiss the correlation. They start blaming gun laws, violent video games, terrorism, mental health of the perpetrator and what not.

Never stop taking your depression medicine without your doctor's permission. If you need to stop taking your medicine for some reason, your doctor may want to reduce your dose gradually. If you stop suddenly, you could have side effects and your depression could get worse. Don't stop on your own; quitting abruptly can lead to symptoms associated with discontinuing a drug as well as risk for relapse.

During the past few years, the global pharmaceutical industry has significantly decreased its investment in new treatments for depression, bipolar disorder, schizophrenia, and other psychiatric disorders. [11]

Some large companies, such as GlaxoSmithKline, have closed their psychiatric laboratories entirely. Others, such as Pfizer, have markedly decreased the size of their research programs. Yet others, such as AstraZeneca, have brought their internal research to a close and are experimenting with external collaborations on a smaller scale. [12]

The retreat is happening despite increased cases of disability due to mental disorders. Despite producing the blockbuster drugs which helped pharma earn billions of dollars, they are retreating. This withdrawal reflects a widely shared view that the underlying science remains immature and that therapeutic development in psychiatry is simply too difficult and too risky.

6. Understanding the Mind

There is a reason why modern medicine is not able to solve any of the health related problems of the mankind. The missing puzzle in finding a solution for any of the mental illness is MIND. There is not an iota of doubt that there is no science of the mind known to the medical world. Science has defined mind as a manifestation of brain. For science, matter is the only reality. Anything which is invisible cannot be present. That is the reason why many psychiatrists don't believe in the concept of soul. Science is only of the matter hence the obsession with the brain.

So, what is the alternative? To really understand the "WHY" of mental health, we must first understand what mind really is and how it works. If you don't understand the mind, you will never be able to improve the health of your mind. Mind is the invisible part of you. Nobody can see and read your mind. It cannot be seen by a CT scan or an x-ray.

If you really look into the human body, brain is only a part of the body. It is no more important than a liver or a heart. In fact, you can be alive with a dead brain but not with a dead heart. But science has denied everything which is not matter. That is the main reason why science is still struggling to understand life. They are looking for reasons in human brain, but there is nothing that can be found there. Brain is like hardware while mind is the software. The brain is designed for survival and it works day in day out to maintain body's homeostasis. It cannot make you smart in anyway. It is our mind which really makes the difference.

If you really want to understand the power of mind (not brain), then read further. You must have heard about – PLACEBO EFFECT. Do you really understand what it is? The word "placebo" comes from Latin which means "I shall be pleasing." "I shall please" hints the kind of treatment done since the early 1700s when there was hardly any proper medicine. Doctors understood the power of placebo and administer fake medicine (just to please people) to improve people's symptoms. A placebo is anything that seems to be a "real" medical treatment - but isn't.

When a patient gets better by ingesting a sugar pill, medicine defines it as placebo effect. It could be a pill, a shot, or some other type of "fake" treatment.

What all placebos have in common is that they do not contain an active substance meant to affect health. In medical research, placebos are used as controls against which the effects of new drugs are measured. So, in simple terms it means an effect caused by our beliefs (that I have taken an actual medicine). Please note that in a research, volunteers are not told if they are taking the placebo or an actual drug.

In the medical schools every student learns, at least in passing, that the mind affects the body. They get a breezy idea that some people get better when they believe (falsely) they are getting a medicine. I am not surprised why the medical community has not called it a mind effect instead of placebo effect. Placebo "masquerades" the actual meaning of the effect, beautifully. Placebo effect is an amazing proof that our mind effect matter (body). I have written about this topic in detail in my book: Why we get sick?

Bruce Lipton is a stem cell biologist. In his best-selling book, *Biology of Belief* he says, "I celebrate the belief effect, which is an amazing testament to the healing ability of the body/mind. However, the "all in their minds" placebo effect has been linked by traditional medicine to, at worst, quacks or, at best, weak, suggestible patients. The placebo effect is quickly glossed over in medical schools so that students can get to the real tools of modern medicine like drugs and surgery." Researchers have found that placebos can work just as well as potent drugs, and studies into the placebo effect have also shown that many conventional treatments "work" because of the placebo effect and little else.

There was a study done by Oxford, Cambridge and Hamburg Universities and the research was later published in the prestigious Science Translational Medicine in the year 2011. The study has shown how placebo or your belief helps your body to recover irrespective of the drug given. In other words, if you believe that you have been given a pain killer; your own brain cells will release such strong opioids which would heal your pain. In this study, patients under severe pain irrespective of the cause, were given strong painkillers (morphine) but were told that this is not morphine but a new vitamin which will not relieve you of your pain but help cure the disease.

Not a single patient got pain relief. Then they took that patient to study the other side and ran saline (salt water) drip and told the patient this is morphine and it will cure your pain. Everybody's pain went away. To understand this anomaly, researchers did a Functional MRI to see what was going on in the brains of these patients. They found that when the patient believed he was administered a painkiller (when he wasn't), the forebrain produced strong Opioids (much stronger than morphine), the pain got less. When patient didn't believe it was morphine (when it was morphine), FMRI showed that the forebrain slept and nothing happened. Patient's pain didn't go away. (Sci Transl Med. 2011 Feb 16; 3(70))

The study backs up the idea that the placebo response plays a role in all treatments for pain, says neuroscientist Fabrizio Benedetti of the University of Turin, Italy. "It seems like magic, the fact that just thinking or believing that you're getting some treatment or benefit can have actual benefits."

Similarly, many other such studies have been done. Even though placebos contain no real treatment, researchers have found they can have a variety of both physical and psychological effects. Participants in placebo groups have displayed changes in heart rate, blood pressure, anxiety levels, pain perception, fatigue, and even brain activity. These effects point to the brain's and as well as our beliefs role in health and well-being. Our brain and body responds to our beliefs.

Henry ford once said about the power of mind or belief, "Whether you believe you can do a thing or not, you are right." You might have seen people walking on burning coals without burning their feet. There are also parallelly numerous incidences where people have burnt themselves. Is it their belief that they can do it which causes little to no damage?

In 1951, Dr. Albert Mason was a young anaesthesiologist at Queen Victoria Hospital in East Grinstead, who in his practice often used hypnotism to treat pain and cure common ailments. Mason has not only treated other patients but in one of his interviews also said. "I thought I'd become an anaesthetist. And during that period of training I experimented with the use of hypnotism for the delivery of babies and delivered about 20 babies by using hypnosis as the only anaesthetic, feeling that that wouldn't anesthetize the baby."

A teenage patient whose skin was so ravaged that after two unsuccessful skin surgeries, his plastic surgeons agreed they could do nothing else to help him. Most of the boy's body - everything but his face, neck, and chest - was covered in a "black leathery skin that Mason said, "felt as hard as a normal finger-nail, and was so inelastic that any attempt at bending resulted in a crack in the surface, which would then ooze blood-stained serum." On the acknowledgment from the plastic surgeon, Dr. Albert Mason tried to treat a young boy's warts with Hypnosis.

Mason in his first session focussed on right arm. Mason hypnotised the boy and in that hypnotic phase, fed him the thought that the skin on that arm would completely heal and would become pink and soft. Within 8 days after this session, the boys' right-hand skin became 90% healed. From a black and armour-like casing, the skin became pink and soft within a few days. Excited with the result, Mason took the boy to his surgeon. The surgeon was shocked to see the result. It is in this moment Mason came to know that the boy was not suffering from warts, but from a lethal genetic disease congenital ichthyosis. By reversing the symptom of a genetic disease just by the power of mind, Mason and the boy had accomplished which was believed to be impossible. Mason later accepted that his belief of treating the boy shook a little after knowing that he was not treating a bad case of warts, instead an untreatable disease. In further hypnotic sessions, the boy's full body recovered by almost 75% though the effect of the subsequent sessions kept decreasing.

Excited by results, Dr. Manson published an article in the British Medical Journal in 1952 with the details of the experiment with the photographs as the evidence. He became an instant star among the patients of similar conditions.

How is it possible for mind to override a genetic programming? How can a doctor's belief that he can treat a patient, affect the later outcomes?

There was an interesting research published on BBC news titled 'Fake alcohol' can make you tipsy', researchers found that simply the belief that you are drinking alcohol (but actually u got tonic water) can cause intoxication and impair judgement. Irving Kirsch, associate director of the Program in Placebo Studies at Harvard Medical School, says this is completely plausible. "When we expect to experience something, that expectation tends to engender, to some extent, that which is expected," Kirsch says. "If we expect to feel pain, that's going to make the pain feel worse ... the stronger we have that conviction, the greater the effect is."

Jeffrey Mogil, the McGill University pain researcher explains, "The placebo effect is the most interesting phenomenon in all of science. It's at the precise interface of biology and psychology."

Do you now understand the power of your mind? Not only it can heal you, it also has power to make you sick. Some studies have shown that almost 90% of your visit to doctor is due to stress.

Where is your mind? We often hear about the word 'mind' but we rarely understand its meaning and power. Some people believe that the mind is in the brain while some say that the mind is different from the brain. The mind is the most powerful and complex tool in the world. No one has really understood what a mind is especially the western audience!

Thoughts are a by-product of the mind. Thoughts cannot be a by-product of the brain; it has to be of the mind. We spend hours in a gym or parks training our bodies but very little in training our most valuable resource - our minds.

The generic English word 'MIND' doesn't do anything. When you say the word 'brain', it creates a set of images for us to understand. We can visualize the shape, color. We can understand how neurons wire and fire. We can understand how brain help maintains our body's homeostasis.

Brain brings along with it the picture of what we are talking about. Similar is not the case with the word 'Mind'. Mind as such doesn't bring any images. Science believes that the mind is the manifestation of the physical brain, hence can be treated by medicines and drugs. If we just forget all the nonsense and look closely, we can find out that mind is not a physical thing. There is no organ which we can call mind in our body. A mind is a made up of thoughts. Thoughts are like clouds. Right now, there may be some thoughts passing by your mind. Thoughts generally don't occur in isolation; they often occur in a bunch. You cannot have one thought and stop. It rarely happens. In fact, some estimates say that we have nearly 70,000 thoughts in a day!

These 70,000 trails of thoughts give us an impression of a mind. A mind is thoughts. To understand the mind, we need to understand thoughts.

Only source where I could find some really good understanding of mind was through the study of spiritual texts and listening to some of the spiritual gurus. Indian yogic system defined the body as comprised of a mental body and a physical body. There was not much importance given specifically to the brain. The yogic system looks at the mind as four fundamental parts.

1. **Intellect or Buddhi**: Buddhi can be defined as the faculty of reasoning and understanding. Buddhi is the logical dimension of thought. Intellect is like a sharp scalpel in the hand of the doctor. Intellect can cut through anything to understand the details of it. If you give a flower to the intellect, it will break down the flower into petals and even further open it up to understand what a flower is. You might get some intricate details about the flower but the flower is no more. You have destroyed the flower. You cannot understand something by destroying it. Unfortunately, the modern education systems and modern sciences have

largely limited themselves to buddhi. "That is a buddhu (foolish) way of existence," says Sadhguru Jaggi.

Buddhi or the intellect cannot function without a certain bank of memory or data. Depending upon the data you have gathered in your lifetime, your intellect plays around with it. If I wipe out all your gathered information, you will look pretty dumb. Isn't it so? To understand this further, look at a 5-year-old. He or she has a brain but you will never take an advice from the kid. Why? Because we value experience. We value data.

Unfortunately, in today's systems of education and academics, buddhi determines everything. If you can make more things out of it, you are considered intelligent, which is not true – you only have a sharp intellect.

2.   **Identity or Ahankara**: You might have heard the term – 'I dentity Crisis'. Identity is a part of our mind which encompasses whatever we relate ourselves to. Identity can be with your family, nation, religion, society, community etc. Now we have also started identifying ourselves with diseases. You can be an Indian, a Bipolar, and an Artist. This is your identity. Your intellect works around your identity. Does this make sense? Let me clarify. Say, if you are only concerned about your religious identity, however sharp intellect you got, it will only work around to protect your identity. It cannot work against it. That is why it's very important to understand how a person is identified. Who are you, is a good question to help you realize what you are identified with.

This is where psychiatry is playing with our minds by giving us new identity or labels. Those labels become our foundation. We continuously look for labels – degrees, professional designations, and accomplishments. I have seen people proudly call themselves as depressed. We call ourselves ADHD, OCD, ADD, Bipolar etc. Due to the identity crisis, we are latching on to any label which give us some identification in this world. We also defend these labels against critics and well wishers. If I tell someone that mental disorder is a fake diagnosis, I have seen people becoming really defensive about their illness as if it is a treasure. They don't want to leave their identity.

Identity is like the hand of the doctor holding the scalpel (our intellect). The steadier the hand, the better the cut. The problem with the present generation is that it has not meticulously worked on its identity. The smaller the group we identify ourselves, the smaller will be our identity. A sharp Buddhi cannot help you unless you identify with the whole world. Without a well-defined identity, a sharp intellect is really painful. We suppress our intellect through alcohol, drugs, eating sugar etc.

Since you are not able to hold the sharp scalpel, it's better to drop it. This identity can also sometimes be called your ego or 'I'. The smaller and the smaller the identity we create, the more destructive we will get. We will not worry about nature, the trees, and the rivers simply because we are not identified with them. All we care is about our family and our survival. In the name of religion and nation, we have done so many idiotic things with pride, simply because our intellect is protecting our identity and what we are identified determines our actions.

Highly educated people have taken up terrorism in the past. Why? Intellect was sharp, but the identity was limited to only religion. A limited identity with a sharp intellect can be a deadly combination. Global warming, polluting rivers, massive deforestation, the killing of animals is nothing but our intellect working for our needs and survival. You will throw garbage on a road if you are only concerned about yourself and don't identify yourself with the whole cosmos. Remember, whatever you are identified with, your intellect works to protect that. Your thoughts, actions, will indirectly be originating from your identity or belief system.

Identity is who we really are. You can be identified to any particular brand. If you believe that you are sick, you have the power to attract diseases.

3.   **Memory or Manas**: The next dimension of the mind is called manas, which is a huge volume of memory. You might not remember your great-great-great-grandfather, but his nose; his eyes are sitting on your face. The heap of memory is carried forward from generation to generation. There is a memory in your body, more memory than you can imagine. It knows about your earliest ancestors. What we call memory is our capacity to remember. But isn't that belittling the whole idea? Memory is contained in each and every cell of our body.

Karmic memory, conscious memory, unconscious memory, evolutionary memory like this there are many types of memory. The body carries the memory of everything that has happened on this planet. If you eat bread, it becomes a human being in a matter of a few hours. A mango seed planted next to a lemon seed will never mistakenly give birth to a lemon tree. Nature never makes a mistake. As you sow, so shall you reap. You can eat a fish and even a fish can eat another fish, but these memories will never accidentally turn a bigger fish into a human being.

When we mention memory, we think about the memory contained in our head. No. Our cell contains trillion times more memory then what we can keep in our head.

Your intellect will look good only because we are feeding it with a lot of information. Without memory your intellect will look stupid especially in the present world. What is in the brain is intellect, not intelligence. Intelligence and memory are right across your body. But people have never been trained how to use this intelligence.

Your memory will be as good as your awareness. If you forget where you have kept your key chain, then next time try to be more aware when you are keeping the key chain at any place. The reason why we have poor memory is because we live our lives in unawareness. There is no problem with your brain.

4.   **Chitta or Cosmic Intelligence**: This is the dimension which is untouched by memory. It is the source of the creation. The people who

have been able to touch this dimension have understood the whole creation. Chitta is always on – whether you are awake or asleep. Your intellect comes on and goes. Many times it fails even when you are awake. If chitta or the intelligence within you was not always on, you could not stay alive. Try to conduct your breath with your intellect – you will go crazy. Chitta is the last point of the mind. It connects to the basis of creation within you.

It connects you with your consciousness. The idea of Chit Shakti is not to keep asking for things. The idea is that if the physical arrangements of life happen easily, you can dedicate more time for your spiritual wellbeing. If you touch this dimension of your mind, which is the linking point to one's consciousness, you do not even have to wish for anything, you do not have to dream of anything – the best possible thing that can happen to you will anyway happen.

The main intention behind this is that your physical life happens more easily, that it does not take your entire time to handle it so that you will have time to close your eyes and sit. Please make use of it for this purpose. Chit Shakti is about touching the dimension of your mind that is pure intelligence – unsullied by memory, unsullied by identification. It is beyond Identity, beyond Buddhi, beyond judgment, beyond divisions – simply there, just like the intelligence of existence that makes everything happen. If you access this, you do not have to worry about what happens or what does not happen. It will happen in a way that you never imagined possible.

That is what happens when you see people posting videos on YouTube of people manifesting dream car or dream house even though they didn't have enough money to afford them at the first place. Once you have access to this unconscious part of the mind, you have the universe working as your partner.

What are thoughts?

"We are shaped by our thoughts; we become what we think"

- *Buddha*

Let me start by sharing a story narrated by Sachinandana Swami. In the capital city of a small kingdom in India, once there lived a Vanika (merchant) who was a very close friend of the King.

On one occasion, the King rode in his chariot followed by his royal entourage, and the regal ensemble headed for the street where the merchant lived. As the royal procession was passing by, the merchant rushed out of his house to greet his friend the King. Their eyes met and they courteously exchanged smiles; but within the King's mind, a little hatred manifested itself.

Upon arriving at his palace, the King immediately called for his very trusted and faithful minister who was also highly intelligent.

The King sadly revealed to the minister about the momentary ill feelings he experienced towards His friend the merchant.

He then commissioned his minister to find the reason why.

So on the next day, the minister set out to pay the merchant a visit during the midday lunch break. The merchant was delighted to receive the minister and since it was lunchtime, he fittingly asked the minister to join him for a meal, as it was tradition to welcome an "atithi" (an uninvited guest).

After having lunch, the minister went to the backyard of the merchant's house to wash his hands and mouth. Whilst performing his ablutions, he caught sight of a huge pile of expensive sandalwood. Returning back into the house, the minister enquired from the merchant about the sandalwood, upon which the merchant expressed his disappointment.

It had been an enormous capital investment, which on account of its high price, the merchant had not found a customer and so the costly item of investment remained untouched for a long time.

It could only be sold when the King dies, for it would be used to cremate His body.

The intelligent minister said, "Have no fear, I shall relieve you of your burden immediately by buying it all." He then quickly took away all the sandalwood and subsequently ordered the Royal Treasury to pay the merchant in full.

The explanation is that when the merchant saw his friend the King during the royal procession, he thought of his precious sandalwood and for an instant, he unintentionally wished for the untimely death of the King. It was for this reason that the King felt ill will towards his dear friend the merchant.

It was a simple exchange of bad vibrations – unwanted bad thoughts which almost ruined a valuable friendship.

Thoughts are like guests - Special guests. Even after they have left, their aura remains and it can have an impact on your body and others. It is best to watch which thoughts you allow in and entertain, and which ones you show the door the moment they turn up.

What is the fastest thing on this planet? No, it's not the Bramhos missile or any stealth plane. It's your thoughts! Your thoughts are so fast that within a split second you can be in Singapore or US or even Moon. Your thoughts can also time travel. It can take you in to the past events and time and possesses the power to foresee the future. Nothing is more important than the thoughts you hold in the mind.

Every one of us has thoughts. Is there anybody who is completely thoughtless? Are you conscious that right at this moment there are thoughts in you? Are thoughts not there from the moment you wake up till the moment you fall asleep? Do you not from morning till evening complain about your own thoughts? You complain that you are worried, anxious, or unhappy. Aren't these emotions, your own thoughts? If yes then you are no stranger to thoughts.

What is a thought? If I ask you, your answer would be probably: a thought just comes. But you have never thought what a thought is. In order to get a clear understanding of the mystery called thought, you must take the time to observe your thoughts. No one really knows what thought is. Is it electrical energy or some other form of energy?

A thought cannot be without an object. You can try. Take a moment and think about anything you want but there should be no object involved. Think! You cannot. Without an object – with a name or form, there can never be a thought. Wherever there are no thoughts as in deep sleep, there are no objects. Every thought hangs on an object.

If I say the words: **Elephant**, **Dog**, **Cat**, **Rat**, **Table**, and **Chair**, what happens? When you read these words, isn't it true that the respective objects came into your thoughts? Either you relate to the meaning of the word or the image of the object pops in your mind. I am sure you were not thinking of an elephant until you read 'Elephant'. The moment that sound or symbol came, there comes a thought. All the objects in the world don't become your thought unless you become CONSCIOUS of an object. When you read the word – Elephant, you become conscious of Elephant.

So what is thought? It is an object plus consciousness. Conscious of an object is a thought.

Object + Consciousness = Thought

Now if I say the words: 'Kidertly', 'Bergitham', what happens? Actually, I just made those words up! Since there was no object (at least your memory is not aware of), there was no thought. It was only awareness which lingered around for few seconds.

Apart from thoughts linked to object, you must also realize that thoughts are past. It cannot be anything else. You cannot think anything which you already don't know. It has to be a permutation and combination of the data you have. That is why it is so hard to get out of your patterns.

The reason why placebo effect works is because we have positive thoughts of belief around it. Negative thoughts are the reason why we experience anxiety. Let me explain. Suppose you are walking on the road on a dark night and you see a snake like figure on the road? Fear grips me. My heart rate increases, I start running backwards. When I finally come to my senses, I might realize that what I assumed as snake was actually a rope. What really happened? A simple thought of a snake caused my body to move from homeostasis to fight and flight mechanism. Body simply reacts to your thoughts even though those thoughts are false. The snake suddenly became real. The body took over. The body can be deceived. The body cannot know whether it is real or unreal, particularly with sex. If you think about it, your body thinks that it is real.

Stress is simply negative thoughts. You might not realize it but if you observe closely, stress is caused by negative thoughts. Anxiety is a condition when you have these negative thoughts run unabated in your head. Depression happens when we remain anxious for a period of time. Do we really understand what happens inside our body when we are experiencing stress?

As soon as your senses perceive danger, hypothalamus releases the hormone CRH (Corticotropin-releasing hormone). This CRH makes a trip to anterior pituitary gland. It binds to the receptors of the target cells and triggers the release of ACTH (Adrenocorticotropic hormone). ACTH then travels through the blood stream to adrenal glands. This ACTH then binds to the cells in the adrenal cortex. It releases multiple hormones including cortisol, adrenaline. Cortisol & adrenaline then triggers multiple responses including ramping up your blood pressure, releasing energy by pumping glucose into your blood, **shutting down non-emergency services like digestion, immune system and egg and sperm development**. Some of you might be thinking why immune, right? Well our body is smart. When it is given an option to choose between being alive or catching a cold, it knows the priority. It knows it can handle flu later as well. These hormones keep racing throughout your body. When our hypothalamus gets a signal that the stressful situation is gone, it stops releasing CRH which in turns stop the ACTH secretion. This further alerts other glands to stop secreting their hormones. Since this communication between glands is hormonal and not electrical like nervous system, it takes some time before your body return to normal. I am sure you must have noticed that it takes some time for your heart beat and breathing to come back to normal; since those hormones linger in the blood stream before being broken down by enzymes.

Imagine that just by having a thought of danger can cause so much activity inside your body. When body is feeling stress, it stops digestion. That's why when we are tensed, we don't feel hungry. I have written about stress in my book: *Why we get sick?*

There is a storm running in your head all the time.

When storm is not there, still sea is there. When storm is not there, there is quietness. We never say that the storm is quiet. Storm simply ceases to exist. The mind is like a storm in your consciousness. When the mind is not there, there is only quietness. There is only awareness. It is the storm of thoughts, which disturbs you. The mind is the disconnect between your body and consciousness. When your thoughts are racing you even forget about your own body. Have you ever encountered a situation when you are driving and suddenly you notice that you have already crossed your destination? If yes, you know that mind can take you away from the reality even the real you.

Still we are day in and day out serving the mind. We are doing everything by the mind, of the mind and for the mind. We spend our entire life and then realize that how stupid was the quest. No wonder the dying have so many regrets. You will regret only when you have done something in unawareness. Isn't it? We react in fit of anger and then go around saying sorry. We use the words – "Sorry, I didn't mean to say that". What do these words tell you? Does it not mean that you were not yourself in those moments when you said nasty words? Who were you then? You were the mind!

In the next chapter, we will try to understand what BELIEFS are.

77

7. Beliefs divides us

What are beliefs? Beliefs are any information which we assume to be true. We don't know if it is true but for us that becomes our truth. Beliefs may not be the actual truth. Although we may not realize but we all have thousands of beliefs about almost everything. Mind you, we love our beliefs. That is the foundation on which we are made from childhood.

Let's start by introspecting on a very basic question. Who are you? You might tell me your name and what you do for a living but that will not be the right answer. Your name and your work are not your decisions. Most of us are doing things which we never wanted to do but we keep doing to live the materialistic life we aspire. Most of us are carrying names, which we would have never wanted to have.

Who are you, really? You are a combination of past, prejudices, beliefs, experiences, conditioning of the society you have grown up in. Even if you change your name or job you will remain the same person.

"When you talk, you are only repeating what you already know. But if you listen, you may learn something new." - Dalai Lama. If you look carefully, you will realize that your thoughts are nothing but who you are and what you already know.

When such is the case, why is there such importance given to thoughts? Your beliefs, upbringing is unique to you. Your thoughts and biases will be unique to you as well. Sometimes we can have a difference of opinion on the same subject. You might feel a particular person is good while someone else might feel differently. Your thoughts are based on what you BELIEVE. It can be a truth or it might not be the truth. It might be just a belief. Why? For knowing the truth, you have to let go of all your information about the past, isn't it? If you take what you already know and try to find the truth about something, you are doing something wrong.

Once there was a wise Monk. People from all over the world came to seek his counsel and advice. One day an important person came to him for learning meditation. He proudly told the monk that he was an influential person and knows a lot of things already. He needs little guidance from the monk to achieve a "meditative state".

The monk smiled and said that they should discuss the matter over a cup of tea. When the tea was served the master poured his visitor a cup. He poured and he poured and the tea rose to the rim and began to spill over the table and finally onto the robes of the wealthy man. Finally, the visitor shouted, "Enough. You are spilling the tea all over. Can't you see the cup is full?" The monk stopped pouring and smiled at his guest. "You are like this tea cup, so full that nothing more can be added. Come back to me when the cup is empty. Come back to me with an empty mind."

You cannot understand anything new unless you forget what you already know, isn't it? You cannot understand people unless you leave behind your previous stereotypes or dogmas. That is why we have a concept called 'unlearning'. Unless you are ready to give up your biases, you cannot think differently.

Have you ever noticed people debating with each other on a topic? Did you ever saw one person convincing the other to agree to one's point? Do people give away their beliefs through debates or pressure? If you introspect, the more someone tries to prove your thoughts are wrong, the stronger will you try to defend yourself. Even if we realize we are wrong, very few will have the guts to admit they are wrong. Why? Because what we believe or have experienced is our truth. If someone brings any point contrary to our beliefs, we tend to become defensive.

A person can have a very different experience while visiting any tourist place. For a person who has a negative experience will think that that is the truth about that place. For person who had a pleasant experience will believe that this is the truth about that place. If the two people meet they will fight out based on their own experience of truth. None of them is correct, isn't it? That is why we have a word called 'stereotype'. Stereotype is a simplified belief about something.

How do thought arise? Have you ever noticed that? One thing is for sure that our thoughts have a mind of their own. As soon as we wake up, we can notice the thoughts racing. Thoughts are always working as a chain. One thought immediately attract another one. This process happens so fast that it's very difficult to even imagine. Even if you imagine something about the unseen future, it will be a projection of your past. It can never be anything beyond what you already know.

What is the mind? A mind is such chains of thoughts. When thoughts are not there, there is no mind as well. When you are not thinking, you are simply aware of what is happening around you. That precisely is what listening is. Listening means that when someone is talking, we shouldn't be thinking. It's such a simple concept yet writers have been writing philosophies on the art of listening. We don't listen properly because we are constantly thinking while someone else is talking. You can turn any machine on or off – but you cannot turn your mind off. There is no switch. So from the moment we reach the age of 4 till our death, the mind continues chattering. No one really knows how to stop thinking. We talk about creativity but can creativity come without rest? We don't know how to rest our mind and the mind is working nonstop. How can creative ideas come in such a case?

On an average day, we have around 70,000 thoughts. That averages to approximately 60 thoughts in a minute. Most of us might simply reject this number as not true. If you take out some time every day and sit with our eyes closed, you will realize how fast your thoughts are happening. Your mind is always active. Even when we sleep, the mind goes on chattering. How? Have you heard about dreams? Dreams are a manifestation of your mind. A mind which is not at rest continues even when your body is no more active. If you are tired of night dreams, you are suffering from your own mind.

When the child is born he has no mind; there is no chattering going on inside of him.

We are slaves to our beliefs and conditioning. A terrorist doesn't feel that he is wrong in any way. His information and conditioning validate his action. He is ready to kill without any sense of guilt. He believes strongly in his information. You cannot debate with a terrorist. You cannot convince him what he is doing is wrong. If you try to that, you are directly hitting his very foundation on which his whole life is based. His foundation is based on the truth that the non-believers are against his religion. If you try to shake people's beliefs, they are going to backfire.

Beliefs divide us. That is why it is so difficult for people to work in corporates. You must have heard experts saying that intelligent people cannot work together. But, do the experts really understand why? Do you understand why it is so difficult for human being to work together? If you understand that, you can also understand why there are so many divorces around the world.

From childhood we are taught to compete with your peers. We fight with each other for the top rank in class. Top rankers are treated entirely different from their peers who are average or below average. There is a component of mind which takes a boost when somebody praises you. You can call it Ego or the feeling of 'I'. The same ego also takes a fall when someone criticizes you. All our education is designed to compete with one other. Even to get the job, you have to battle it out with your peers. Now when we come to corporate culture, we are told to cooperate and work as a team. When those high rankers come together there is bound of be the clash of egos.

Religions are just beliefs. Beliefs are personal truths, not the real truth. I believe in Christianity or Buddhism or Islam. I have not seen or heard for myself what Buddha or Christ or Mohammad told. I simply believe what others are talking or reading as truth. I believe what is written in the bible as fact. None of that has been my experience yet. Even if I read a bible a thousand times, I am simply repeating what has been written there. Nothing has been in my experience.

Memorizing something mean that you didn't understand. We all know what I mean. We all have passed examinations by simply mugging textbooks. If you really understood what is written in the book, you would never need to memorize anything. Those who quote exact verbatim from a book are indirectly telling that they didn't understand anything. They are just repeating what someone influential said in the past.

Sadly there is certain religious interpretation that has created more violence than anything in this world. People are ready to die for what they believe.

Having beliefs is convenient as we don't have to do anything to know the truth for ourselves. Unless I experience the truth myself, such knowledge is useless. It will not bring any transformation in your life. We have beliefs for nearly everything. We would have stereotypes about everything.

We have beliefs about our government, country, neighbours, society, religions, languages, health, money, children, marriage, family, cars, brands, clothes, etc. The list can go on and on and on. Beliefs are for the lazy ones. People who have fear of the unknown resort to beliefs. Beliefs make our life more secure. It gives us the perception that we know. But what we know is really half-baked reality. Alexander Pope (1688-1744) once said, "A little knowledge is a dangerous thing."

Half knowledge becomes dangerous when you actually assume that you know enough to take a decision. Half knowledge in medicine, drugs, chemistry, business, engineering, and in other similar disciplines is too dangerous. When we are afraid of death, we believe in concepts of the afterlife.

Beliefs divide us. Their innate feature is division. Cooperation is only possible if everyone believes in the same thing, isn't it? We expect people to respect minorities, other religious beliefs, other sexual preferences. How will that ever happen? Unless we can break people's long held beliefs, we can never achieve true peace and communion in our world.

But remember that all we have is beliefs. If you touch my beliefs, you are inviting resistance. If you use force, you will further strengthen my resolute and my beliefs. Terrorism is one of the major side-effects of belief system; belief that my religion is better than yours, believe that people following other religions must die.

Let me take you back to Indian history. The year was 1984 when Prime Minister Indira Gandhi was assassinated.

History remembers the operation called Operation Blue Star. Operation blue star tells us how easy it is to influence people in the name of religious beliefs. Before we go into operation blue star, let's try to understand why the partition of India took place in 1947 post independence. Partition was done based on beliefs; belief that Muslims cannot live safely with Hindus. Muslims wanted to have a separate country for them. Millions died as a direct result of this partition.

In 1971, Pakistan's army was creating havoc in Bangladesh and India intervened. India helped to make Bangladesh (part of Pakistan after independence) an independent nation. Pakistan was humiliated by the loss. In retaliation, Pakistan started planning to break India. The plan was to incite another religion based partition. This time they bribed and helped certain sects of Sikhs to demand their own religion specific country.

Many Sikhs started the demand for Khalistan (a separate country for Sikhs). The plan was to create panic and fear among the Hindus in Punjab and force them to flee from the state. This was the similar strategy used by Pakistan in the Indian state of Jammu and Kashmir to flee the Kashmiri Pundits.

Now come back to 1984. Backed by Pakistan, militant religious leader Jarnail Singh Bhindranwale gathered inside a prominent religious place called Golden temple. They were planning to launch a final massive attack on Hindus and finally fled to Pakistan (whose border was only 10 km from that place).

Intelligence Bureau reported that weapons training were being provided at gurdwaras in Jammu and Kashmir and Himachal Pradesh. Soviet intelligence agency KGB reportedly tipped off the Indian agency RAW about the CIA and ISI working together on a plan for Punjab.

RAW from its interrogation of a Pakistani Army officer received information that over a thousand trained Special Service Group commandos of the Pakistan Army had been dispatched by Pakistan into the Indian Punjab to assist Bhindranwale in his fight against the government. A large number of Pakistani agents also took the smuggling routes in the Kashmir and Kutch region of Gujarat, with plans to sabotage. [1]

The then Prime minister finally decided to handover Punjab to the Indian army. Since the militants with dangerous weapons were hiding in Golden temple, Indira Gandhi decided to send the army to the gurudwara. The code word for the operation was Blue Star. Bhindranwale was expecting that army or police will never dare to enter the religious place. Religion is such a strong force!

Few journalists including Satish Jacob met Bhindrawale in Golden temple. Bhindrawale declared that he will fight in case the army takes any action. Army will be given a proper response. Army made a constant appeal to the militants to come out and surrender but their voice fell on deaf ears.

Operation blue star began on 5th June 1984 at 7 pm. After two days the militant leader Bhindranwale was found dead. In the Blue star operation, 83 army personnel lost their lives. 492 militants were killed in the operation although people claim that many more innocent people were also killed. After the search operation, the army found a huge collection of arms and ammunitions including anti-tank rocket launchers.

Do you see the power of beliefs and religion? In fact, religion and belief are not different. Did the militancy reduce after the operation blue star? No. The force to suppress beliefs can make the belief even more strong. The militancy continued. In the operation blue star, the religious gurudwara was damaged. Sikhs were hurt. Nobody was now concerned if what army did was good for the country. Religion was more visible to people. The burnt religious books and damaged buildings were more visible.

After a few months in Oct, Indira Gandhi was assassinated by her own Sikh security guards. I don't want to tell you who was right or who was wrong. Let's not even bother about that. Let's look and introspect that we lost many precious lives. For what? For some religious beliefs?

Punjab lost many years of growth and development. It took more than a decade to finally suppress the militancy after the 1984 operation.

Come back to 2018. We know how this problem of religion has spread across the world. Terrorism is now a global problem. We hear shooting cases across the United States and Australia. ISIS is now a global threat. I don't want to tell you who were responsible for any of this but if you look at the very base of the problem – it is the religion which can be used to make people do the most idiotic things possible. People are ready to become a human bomb and blow themselves off. Isn't this madness? And let me correct my words. These people are not idiots. They are believers. They have such a strong belief that they are even ready to give up their lives.

8. Religion is an invention of the mind

Any religion, any ideology that is based only on belief, faith, is bound to cripple your intelligence.

- *Osho*

Look around you carefully. What has been the biggest killer of mankind since the beginning of time? If you add the numbers properly, you will definitely find religion in the list of top 3 culprits. Religious beliefs have been the root cause of so many deaths that it is sick to even link it to God. If we really understand history, God didn't create religion, people did. Religion was an easy way of regulating and exploiting people. Religion was used as a tool to create fear and compliance among the masses. Period!

Before you get offended, let's get to the history of the biggest religion in the world. Let us go back in time when it all started.

Do you know how atheism came into the picture?

You might ask, why so much defiance against God or the church among atheists? Well to understand this we must go into mythology and to as early as 4th Century. Western thoughts have originated from the Biblical and Greek mythology. Greek beliefs were based on defiance of the Gods who lived on Mount Olympus.

The goal of Greeks was Elysium, a place meant for people who lived a heroic life. To win a place in Elysium humans had to defy gods. This was the final destination of mythic heroes such as Achilles, Perseus, and Theseus etc. They also believed in one life with urgency to do important things and "I am the authority and I bow down to no one."

The Roman Empire was the extension of this belief. It was this belief which inspired Alexander of Macedonia, in 4th century BCE to conquer the world. For centuries, the Roman Empire was the most extensive political & social structure in western civilization. When the Roman Empire collapsed in the 5th Century, Christianity became the dominating force across Europe. There was a flip from 'defying God' to believing and complying with one all-powerful God.

During the European middle ages, the Catholic churches really dominated the European civilizations. It was almost impossible to imagine the power invested in the Catholic churches in the middle ages. The church owned 1/3rd of all land that made them the most dominant political force/authority in the whole European region. The Pope even claimed authority among all kings in Europe, as a successor to the Roman Empire. The church was the most powerful authority and decided almost every aspect of the civilization. They were deciding the education, feeding the poor, running old age homes, marrying people among many day to day activities. Peasants in return paid Church taxes.

Gullible and poor people were made to believe that it was only through faith and faith alone one can attain salvation. Your good deeds, donations etc. cannot give you any benefits if the faith is forsaken.

Minds of men easily get corrupted. With so much power vested in the Pope, obviously the mind got corrupted. There is a history of evil Popes who committed debauchery, murders and whatnot as no one could dare question them. Sooner or later, such authority was bound to be questioned. Although there was growing dissent among the ways of Church, peasants didn't dare to raise their voice.

A man named Martin Luther rose to the occasion. The theology of Martin Luther was instrumental in influencing the Protestant Reformation, specifically topics dealing with Justification by Faith, the relationship between the Law and the Gospel, and various other theological ideas. Martin outright denied the sole authority of church and its officers. He refuted the age-old claims of the churches and proclaimed that the church and its officers have no spiritual powers. He said that the priesthood was a human invention and that the individual Christians don't even need a priest to receive the grace of God.

In 1532, Luther was called before the emperors to defend his views. Thanks to the printing press, which was introduced at around the same time, Luther was able to spread his words through books, articles, and cartoons. His views reached millions quite fast. The radical viewpoints shined among the oppressed and the suppressed. Prior to Luther, bibles were written only in Latin which the then common population couldn't read. Luther translated and published the Bible in German so that the common population can also have access of Bible in the language they could read.

Luther expected that giving easy access to Holy Scriptures will give people an understanding of the facts. They would realize the fallacy of the present system and how it has been used to exploit them. Once the common population got access to the holy script, they realized different meanings out of the same text. That is how it happens. The same thing can be interpreted in many ways by different people. Luther was expecting that the spread of teachings of the bible would put the church in order, but instead it lead to division of people under several sects.

Based on their understanding of the scripture, Luther's Protestants started creating spin-offs like Anabaptist, Zvinglivs, Puritans, etc. These spin-offs further divided into finer groups; each one thinking that they knew the right way to worship God and the other one is obviously wrong and going to hell.

Finally the people resisted. Peasants took up the ideas of Luther and revolted against the long pending grievances against the landlords and clergyman. Peasants echoed Luther's language proclaiming that the Serfdom was invented by the man with no basis in scriptures. Peasants refused to pay taxes, pillaged church lands and raised an army of 3, 00,000 people. At least 1, 00,000 people died in this struggle.

Soon few kings separated themselves from the Church. Monarchs found this idea very beneficial for themselves. Protestantism allowed them to confiscate Church land and collect Church taxes. That is why the queen is the largest landowner in England - because of protestant revolution. Once again the Greek way was taking birth. The decades and decades of oppression by the Church were being toppled.

Europe was torn between Greek way and the biblical way and later the protestant way and the catholic way. Every 'way' was convinced that the other was wrong and they were right (one truth or my way). The end of Crusades saw the start of a scientific revolution in Europe with the rebirth in the inspiration from the Greek beliefs. Once again, the truth imposed by authorities, kings or Churches were rejected and truth based on evidence was sought. Everything had to be explained in mathematical equations.

Devdutta Pattnaik in his book Business Sutra says," The scientist was the Greek hero on a lone quest, those who opposed him was the Olympian Gods. The scientific spirit inspired discoveries, inventions and industrialization. With scientific exploration, society no longer needed the anchors of faith. Knowledge mattered, not belief!"

Many Protestants made their way to the newly discovered continent of America; the new promised land. It is no surprise that most scientists are proud 'atheists'. So now you may know that atheism is a direct outcome of the oppression of Christianity. People took that anti-God stance because they saw that God has allowed so much destruction. They saw the Pope involved in corruption, predatory activities, and murders. Fooling people in the name of a fake concept called religion was bound to turn off people sooner or later.

Yes. Religion is a fake concept. It was created by man. Jesus didn't create Christianity. He didn't write the bible. Bible was created to fool and dominate common people.

Fooling people in the name of religion is still common in the west. Televangelists, in the name of God, ask a fixed amount of donations as seed money. In lure that, the donator will get back the money from some unknown source multiplied many times over. Oliver showed how the worst televangelists often prey on vulnerable people by tricking them into believing that the more money they donate; the more they will receive from God in return. There are a number of pretty bad televangelists still operating today.

That theory might be true if the money is reaching the needy but it's often revealed that this money was used by some churches and preachers for personal luxuries like buying private jets, houses etc. The even worse thing, televangelists even force people who don't have money to take credit on their credit cards to pay them and believe that by faith God will wipe out their credit debt. There was a real case where televangelists have admitted that God can even heal diseases like tumours and cancers, if the patient would send a cheque of $1000 every month. In one such case, a gullible patient did send out multiple cheques and forsaken real medical treatment which resulted in her death.

A priest or a bishop or a maulana is needed to contact God. Religion is needed to contact God. Osho in his book Learning to Silence the Mind mentioned the fallacy of the whole bureaucracy of the religions. He said, "The pope has even said that this is counted as a sin, to try to have any direct contact with God - a sin! You have to contact God through a properly initiated Catholic priest; everything should go through proper channels."

This is so appalling that in most religions there is a hierarchy. Higher the person in that hierarchy, closer he is to God. You cannot bypass the priest or a bishop and directly enter the God's house. This is not allowed. What an idiotic theory!

Now I am not saying that only Christianity has such a bad history. Other religions have not done any good either. The second largest faith is Islam. Its history is full of blood sheds also. In fact, it's still the most blood shedding religion on earth. Terrorism is a direct outcome of Islamic ideologies like Jihad against non-Muslims. Terrorism is a direct outcome of Religion. People who say the terrorism is not linked to religion are diplomats. They dare not speak the truth.

The whole idea of terrorism has been inspired by the concept of jihad, the religious duty to struggle. Jihad has been associated with violent struggles with non-Muslims. It is not only Islam which is the culprit here. Christianity has a bad history of crimes and exploitation too. Islam and Christianity have been fighting for centuries on this belief system. Both Islam and Christianity have drastic similarity. They only differ in certain beliefs. BELIEFS!

From time and again, divine souls have come to this planet and they reminded everyone of the qualities of a soul - Blissful, loving, Purity, compassionate, knowledgeable, peaceful, and powerful. Jesus, Buddha, Mahavir, Osho, Vivekananda, Guru Nanak all reminded us of our dharma. They all taught us peace, love, honesty, kindness, compassion. Wasn't this the actual message of all these spiritual teachers? Every teacher was teaching us our dharma. Every teacher was teaching us to connect with our real self.

But the tragedy for the human souls - Instead of connecting with their teachings, we connected with the teachers. Instead of becoming a good human being, we became a good Christian, Buddhist, or Muslim. If we would have connected with the teachings, we would have been a united, but we unfortunately focussed more on the messenger then on the message.

Every guru had a slightly different way of telling the same message. Then more teachers came under such divine souls and we became further divided. We converted a Guru into a religion. Humans are responsible for the destructions done by religious beliefs. Today we are killing each other in the name of religion. Our real religion was purity, love and kindness. Today we are fighting whose teacher or guru was better. What a shame!

According to some estimates, there are around 4000 religions in the world. Imagine that! If we simply look at the history of religion, it was used as a tool of suppression. It was indirectly used to make the people subservient to the godly authority. That was the reason that finally the revolution happened in Europe - against the church and the kings. People were fed up with their dominance and excessive meddling in people's lives and decisions.

Here are some questions for you to answer honestly.

1. Can we not live without religion?

2. What has religion given to us?

Animals, trees and all other life forms are able to survive without religion. What has religion given us? Has religion shown us God? How many of your religious forefathers were able to reach God? After death you may say. How do we know if that claim is even correct? Do we just believe anything which is said to us?

Nature has not discriminated us based on religions. If you cut open a body of a Muslim and a Buddhist, there will be no difference. The only difference will be in the mind. Religion is a prison created for us. As soon as a child is born, he is thrown into one or the other cage. We are trapped in our own ideologies. We cannot think sanely. Common sense is absent in the eyes of a Jihadi. People can be forced to do really stupid things in the name of God and religion.

People become a human bomb; attack the innocent to please their God. Did Mohammad write the Quran? Did Jesus write the Bible? Even if you say yes, how do you know if over the decades it has not been modified by kings to suit their agenda, to rule people? Religions have created so much mess in the world including preying on the poor to convert them across religions. There is a race to increase their numbers. Islam allowed Muslims to polygamy and also beautiful virgins after death.

Understand that religions have not done any good for you. They can never do as they are a man-made concept. They are the concepts of mind.

The reason priesthood still exists is because of these complex languages which still exist. Sanskrit is the languages of the priests in India. Since the common people don't speak in Sanskrit there is a constant need for them. All religious text has been written in Sanskrit.

They have made themselves indispensable. We need them as a mediator in reaching to God. This is the reason Buddha used people's language and priests hated him for that. If people can understand the meaning of all the scriptures and shlokas, there is no need of for a priest.

Humans don't need religions. Religion is a very recent development. The caveman lived peacefully without any need of a religion for thousands of years. I am not debating if there is a God or not, all i am saying is that, God cannot be different for you and me. If there was a creator, he or she has to be a single person as most religions practice (monotheism). How is it possible that the two different religions have created different Gods? It is all beliefs. When those prophets lived, they were tortured and killed. Jesus was prosecuted. Stones were thrown at Buddha. Now after thousands of years we have made them equivalent to God. Why? We are ready to kill on slightest provocations in the name of God. Blasphemy might be the most used word recently. People in Pakistan are being given death sentences on the charges of blasphemy.

Imagine a world without religions. Imagine the day when all the temples, churches, mosques have gone. Humans are just what they are meant to be by the creation – HUMAN. All differences, killings, hatred have gone away. Atheism is also not good. We don't need any suspicions in the mind of people about anything. Just be a human with no pro-beliefs and anti-beliefs.

Imagine the amount of money and land that would be available for useful work. God doesn't live in temples or churches.

Organized religions are of no use. There is no practical relevance. If you believe in God, find him for yourself. There is no point of believing something old age and becoming miserable for life. The world will be such a nice place when we can renounce all sorts of beliefs and just focus on ourselves. Be more human. Be more compassionate.

9. Marriages are not made in heaven

Marriages are not made in heaven and the numbers speak. I am always intrigued by the physical concept of hell and heaven. I can understand the idea. The idea is great but it is mostly used by religions to tame the characters of its people. Nearly all religions have the concept of an after death place. Heaven is a place designed to reward people who have done good deeds while hell is a place designed to punish the evildoers. Some religions also believe that those who believe in God have a place in heaven, while Hell is a place for nonbelievers.

There is a brilliant picture painted for all of us about these afterlife places. Heaven has great food, virgins, pleasures, and whatnot. It is a place with the immense beauty of God. Hell is a place with flowing lava, tortured souls, and evil janitors.

If you are one who also believes in any of the above images, remember that it is just a belief. There is no way you have or anyone alive has personally experienced any of this. Heaven and hell are not in your own personal experience. In fact, no living person could ever know what occurs after death. You can argue with people who have an NDE, but again you have to simply believe what that person is saying. It is still not in your own experience. In fact, I have written about NDE in my previous book: *5 life changing lessons from the Near Death Experience of others*. Based on my research and analysis, no one talked about heaven and hell in their experience of near death.

Net-net anybody who is alive and gives logic in favour of hell and heaven has to be a religious believer. He has no proof apart from some text written by someone hundreds of years back. No one even knows who wrote the text and what it really means. People have been drawing different interpretation of the same text from centuries. Christians are divided into so many smaller sects like Catholic Church, Eastern Orthodox Church, Oriental Orthodoxy, Anabaptism, Protestantism, Restorationism and Nontrinitarianism and so many other minor groups. Why? Because each group interpreted the same Bible in different ways.

How can a message be so dicey and political? Mind you that they all have read the same Bible but have drawn different interpretations out of that. Muslims are divided into Shia and Sunni based on different beliefs.

Look at the Indian ancient text of Bhagavad Gita. From centuries, people are drawing different conclusions from the same text. How is it possible? How can Jesus, Krishna, Buddha, Mahavir and Mohammad say things which can be interpreted in 100 ways? Was their narration so poetic? Only Poems can be interpreted in so many ways. There has to be something entirely wrong in the message or the people who interpreted those messages.

For example, most religious books talk about peace, love and harmony yet these religious texts have become the greatest mass murderers of all times. Millions and millions have died and are currently dying because somehow people are still misinterpreting the text written in them. Certain religious leaders used this made up the concept of heaven to entice people to become suicide bombers. Men are fooled to believe that if they do God's work while on earth (often killing the non-believers); they will be rewarded with 72 beautiful virgins!

I once saw a terrorist photographed with a bomb tied all over his body. He had a protective steel case tied around his penis. This guy was planning to protect his penis for the afterlife's heavenly love. If he had used his little brain, he would have known that this body cannot leave this planet after death. Probably it will be blown into pieces.

But, you cannot reason with a religious person. Common sense has to be forsaken when you start believing stuff. Can you reason with that terrorist trying to protect his penis from blowing up? Even if his penis survives, what use it is in the afterlife! Don't you already know that when we die, we leave our physical body behind?

All pleasures of the world belong to your body. It is your tongue which has the capability to enjoy tasty meals. It is your penis which can enjoy sex. Your physical body will rot here on Earth. How are you planning to enjoy delicious meals in heaven? Well, you cannot reason with believers. Believers have already isolated themselves from other logics and truth. They cannot see beyond their veils.

WHY DO WE BELIEVE SO EASILY? If a doctor comes and say to you that this toothpaste is the best, you will believe what he says. Very little we realize that this guy might be taking money from a company to promote their brands and actually toothpaste may have no physical value. That is why multinationals cast actors dressed as doctors in advertising such products. It is easy to fool people by making them believe something. That is also the reason why an advertisement is shown so *many times* a day. It is playing with your belief system, nothing more.

Why it is easy for us to believe? Because there is no effort required to find out the truth. I don't have to spend any time in believing something. A child can believe there is a ghost under his bed in a split second that idea is put in his brain. But slowly and steadily, he will know that truth and will laugh at his own foolishness.

It is clear that heaven and hell are the concepts created by the mind. These concepts are obviously used for various nefarious ends, often to fool people. Often to make them behave morally and control them. Heaven and hell are dependent on your believe and faith. If you have faith in God, heaven will be opened to you, else prepare for hell. Can we become more idiots then this?

Let's come to marriages now. Marriage seems to be a beautiful concept or at least that is how it is painted by most. Two people made for each other. Two people caring and loving each other for their entire life. Like the concept of heaven and hell, marriage is also a man-made concept. It is a direct way to impose morality in men and women. Is it not?

It is a tool to bring a certain order in the society. Certain religions have also put a restriction on how many marriages a person can do, while some religions encourage polygamy. Reproduction is a very casual process in nature. All other life forms are able to reproduce without imposing any morality in the process. Humans although are special. They have made reproduction a very process oriented activity. Men and women must be married in order to reproduce.

Marriages are a social design to trap men and women. This concept doesn't exist in the universe. Nature invented love, we invented marriages. Let's see what marriages have really done for the world.

1. Marriages take away your freedom. Freedom is very dear to us. It is the only thing we long for in our life. Marriages are associated with confinement. You feel trapped. In India, we have a famous saying, "Marriage is such a sweet that those who haven't eaten repent and those who have eaten also repent." Although these words are often used jokingly, there is an innate truth behind them. Marriages are designed to look attractive from outside but only when you have been there you realize that it was better otherwise. Society has painted a picture that when you get married you will be happy.

2. The problem of dowry has been a direct outcome of marriages. Women were supposed to bring money with them to the groom's house. This tradition is pretty common in many parts of the world. Look at the amount of money we spend on marriages! We decorate everything so that marriage will look good. The Indian wedding industry currently accounts for over USD 15 billion dollars and is growing at a rapid rate of 25-30% each year. An average Indian wedding could cost between 20 lakhs to 5 crores. A person in India is estimated to spend one-fifth of the total wealth accumulated in his lifetime on a wedding. Imagine that a country which is still considered poor spends so much money on something which is so irrelevant in their lives.

3. Divorces are a direct outcome of marriages. Every year thousands of people get trapped in the long life alimony payments. Thousands of children get separated from one of their parent. Millions of dollars are spent in court and lawyer fees. Married people, who realize that they have made a mistake, decide to part ways. In India, due to societal pressures, the divorce rate is very low compared to other countries. The pace of divorce in India is about 13 per 1,000 marriages against 500 in 1,000 marriages in the UK. This is not very encouraging news. It is only fear that is stopping many Indians from divorcing their better halves.

4. Prostitution is another direct outcome of marriages. Marriages set the boundary how a man or woman should behave. Indians believe that love will happen automatically after marriage. It rarely happens. Marriages in India are purely for sexual needs, nothing beyond. In western world, there is no such obligation; hence people don't get married even till their late 30s. Arranged marriage concept works because else most men and women would remain unmarried.

When the man didn't find love in the marriage, prostitution was born. Till few decades back, it was only females who were prostitutes. Now we are also hearing about male prostitution. Prostitution will rise because the love that was expected to arise after marriage never took place. That is why prostitution was made legal in many countries. It was done to make sure that family structure remain intact. Marriages remain intact. What can be more immoral than this? We have thrown few women into sufferings so that marriage institution can survive.

5. The subjugation of woman is a direct outcome of marriages. A woman has been treated as third-class citizens since time unknown. After marriage, they were supposed to take care of their new God – husband. Women were supposed to cook food, serve her master with bodily desires and bear children. They were jailed for the rest of their lives.

There was no freedom there. A woman was almost equivalent to slaves. They were not supposed to have any opinions. Oppression of woman was a direct outcome of marriage. The present drives of feminism are an outburst of centuries of slavery.

In Islam, you can still see the slavery of woman. Those black burkas are a symbol of slavery. Slavery to religion and men. Men want to dominate their wives.

Women are now able to break the shackles of this slavery. They can earn a living and voice their opinions. They have proved that they are not meant to be reserved for kitchens. That is also the reason why we are seeing more divorces now than ever. Divorce is an outcome of people who finally saw the fallacy called marriage. Divorce is a liberating concept. If you are not feeling happy and liberated after marriage, why to continue with such bondage.

There is a reason why people in the west are fearful of commitment called marriage. Live in relationship is on the rise. While some might debate this as immoral, these trends are showing that people are losing their trust in the whole institution called marriages. Love has nothing to do with marriage. Love is the most pure emotion which is present in all the life form. People hate lovers. They are happy for their girls to marry a guy whom she doesn't know then to marry her to someone she loves. Love is what holds a family together; else the whole concept of family collapses. It's funny that in India, it is the societal pressure which pushes people to marry. What will people think about a girl who is ageing and is still unmarried?

We cannot blame the society as well. This is what we have been made by our ancestors. Marriage is a concept passed on to us and we all have taken it without question. It is the normal and any one not married is not normal or strange. Osho once narrated a beautiful story around this concept. Once a magician came to a village and put some chemical in the village wells. He claimed that whoever would drink the water from these wells will become mad. By the evening, thirst prompted people to drink water of the wells. They all went crazy. There was a separate well for the king, queen and their ministers. They rejoiced that they were saved from this insanity. By the night, the whole village including the soldiers had accumulated outside the king's palace and they all claimed, "Our king is mad. We have to remove him."

The king and ministers very afraid as a mad person can harm them as well. They decided that in order to save their lives, they must also drink the water from the well in the village. In the mid of the night, they escaped from the secret door of the palace and drank water from the well.

All the villagers rejoiced that their king has become alright. There was a big celebration all night. This is exactly how we the society has made sure that no one should remain sane. Chains of marriages must be used so that people remain bound to the world. The quest to realize one's higher self can be blocked.

Concept of family and children has been erected on the concept of marriage instead of love. It is no wonder that domestic violence has been the part of parcel of every marriage in India. Domestic violence can be physical, emotional, verbal, economic and sexual abuse. Domestic violence can be subtle, coercive or violent. In India, 70% of women are victims of domestic violence. 38% of Indian men admit they have physically abused their partners.

It is no surprise that there is no love in these marriages. Love cannot be born in bondage. Love needs freedom. The reason marriages are failing is because we want to two people to love while in a bondage. How is that ever going to be possible? Yes, two people who love each other can decide to be family but there is no need for a marriage in such a case.

Imagine the children born in such families. They are subjected to violence from a very young age. Parents, who don't love each other, cannot love their children either. Such married women can become a mother but they will never be able to really become a mother. The love for the children will never be there as the child is a constant remembrance of her husband. She or he will beat and scold the child by drawing conclusions as to from whom the child has learned this behaviour. Man will blame the wife for child's negative aspects and so will the woman. You can imagine the mental state of the children and then we blame increasing violence in the society. How are you planning to increase harmony in the world without securing harmony in individual houses?

Without love, our children are getting abnormal. They are going depressed; they are going violent, drug addicts. They are running after sex at a very young age, there is no push to find love. Love is not their cup of tea as they have never known what true love is. They have never seen true love. They are running after physical pleasures. There is a reason why mental diseases are on the rise and marriages have played a crucial role in this regards. Sad part is our preachers will never admit this. Society will never admit this.

Terrorist is a person who has been devoid of love. There is no love left in him. Such soul is ready to break, destroy. Look at the gun shooting incidents in America. Those are bound to increase. People are broken. They are losing their minds. Love was the mould which was supposed to keep them sane, but that mould has long been removed. Man is falling apart. Psychiatry and pharma have spotted this gap. They are targeting the already fallen men and women.

Divorces, violence and dowry numbers are shouting out loud for so many years. But nobody is there is to hear as we have become so mechanical. We see our parents fighting but still repeat the same mistakes they have done. I heard my mom say that she will take divorce many times, obviously in a fit of anger. But she couldn't act since the consequences of that might be even dire. Non-working women are dependent on their husbands.

In fact, marriages were the reason that the middle class parents went ahead and opted for female foeticide. Female foeticide was a big problem so much so that, the Indian government had to pass a law to make it criminal offense for doctors to tell the sex of the foetus. A female child was considered bad as marriages involved lot of money to be paid to the groom's family. Dowry which was a part of marriage was the reason families killed many females, sometimes even after birth.

Women who gave birth to female child were beaten and often treated badly by the husband's family

Many couples decide to have a baby in anticipation that their marriage will improve. Nothing happens. A child is only a distraction. Mother-in-laws and daughter-in-laws are fighting. Mother and mother-in-laws are fighting. Where is the love? Marriages are the center of hatred and animosity yet we fail to see. When a child is born he is so playful and loving. Everyone loves him or her. There is no depression. Depression is a direct result of lack of love. He or she will drink and do drugs to avoid the reality. The reason why alcohol consumption is increasing is directly related to lack of love. The reality is so bad that people want to forget it. What is a better way to feel better than a quick drink or two?

There is a difference between loyalty and forced loyalty. Marriages are a way to enforce loyalty among the social animals. To even idolize marriages, we have linked it to heaven - both concepts created by human mind. Heaven is imaginary and so is marriage.

An emotion which is so important for our lives is shunned but violence is openly encouraged. Children are open to domestic violence, violence in their computer games, violence in entertainment including boxing and WWE. We are open to violence on the streets but if someone is seen romancing on the streets, it's a big problem.

Our society hates people who love. We have been always opposed to lovers. History is filled with stories of lovers who couldn't unite due to society. Even today we hear that a boy was killed by girl's family because they loved each other. A father will not like her daughter to love a man before marriage. A father expects the daughter to love her husband. Love should come after marriage. Lovers have to hide; they are scared to be seen in public.

Net-net we can understand that marriages and heaven are created to force morality down your throats. It is a way to control you. While the concepts might have been thought with a noble intention, their relevance can always be cross-examined in the present world.

10. Fallacy of Desires

There is a proverb in India that says, "When I had all my teeth, I had no nuts to chew and now that I got the nuts, I have no teeth to chew." When Alexander was in India, he used to meet a lot of yogis and saints. He once went to meet a saint who would never wear any clothes. The naked saint was sitting beside a river bathing in the sunlight. After coming close to him, Alexander announced, "Hey saint, you are lucky that Alexander the great has come to meet you."

Saint smiled and said, "A person who calls himself great has to be mad. I have never seen a poor man like you. The claim of being great is to hide the internal poverty of yours. These clothes, jewels, crown, sword, the army is all a grand show-off. Internally you are completely empty."

Alexander smiled. He was always intrigued by the saints of India. He claimed, "You have nothing. You sit here naked and aimless. What do you have which makes you make such statements? I have everything yet you call me poor."

Saint said, "Yes. You have so much yet your desire to gather more hasn't stopped. I have nothing yet I don't have any desires for anything. That is why I am a king and you are a beggar."

Alexander felt a sensation in the answer of the naked saint. He said, "I like your answer but I cannot be like you, at least not in this birth."

Saint smirked. He said, "If you want to become like me, it is so easy. Right here and right now it is possible. Drop your sword, jewels, clothes, and army and lie down on the bank of the river. There is enough space for two of us. To become Alexander requires a lot of effort. To become me you don't have to make any effort.

Alexander said, "I am really impressed meeting you. Now that I am here, can I do anything for you?"

Saint said, "What should I ask you? I don't have any demands or desires. But if you really want to do something for me, I will not let you go feeling sad. If you really want to do something for me, move a little sideways. You are blocking the sun rays.

Alexander felt small in front of the naked saint. He said, "Right now I am on a quest to conquer the world. Once I will be done, I will live the rest of my life like you."

"O, King! The journey you are on is never going to end. No one has ever returned from the journey led by desires. There is no end to it. As soon as you will fulfill one desire, another will pop-up and then another. Death comes before the end of such a journey," said the saint.

Alexander died on his way back. He couldn't even reach home. He died with an unfulfilled desire.

There is something strange about DESIRE. One who is galloping on desires has no peace. A life focussed on desires, can never be a fulfilled life. Even if you desire to have peace, you will miss peace. That is the nature of desires and wants. Have you not noticed this in your life? No matter what you achieve, you will never be satisfied. As soon as one desire gets fulfilled another rises up. Even if you feel you have achieved something great, death will take it away. If you have never noticed this nature of desires, then look carefully next time. I have written about this topic in a separate book – *There is no goal in life*.

Mind is a mechanism of desiring. Mind is always in desire, always seeking something, asking for something. Mind doesn't stops desiring. As soon a kid starts to develop the mind, he or she will constantly demand and desire. Believe it or not, marketing exploits this desiring mind. They bombard us with ideas that if you buy this, you are buying happiness. If you eat this, you will feel like heaven. Mind is easily caught in these desires. Sex, food, materialism are all baits for the mind. Mind runs after them never resting in peace. That is why when someone dies we say "REST IN PEACE". What else can we say? We saw that person running around all his life. Now he can rest in peace. That is the biggest prayer for the dead.

Buddha described desires as the root of all sufferings. There is a reason why. A life filled with desires is equivalent to a bucket without a bottom. When you put the bucket inside the well, it looks filled. But as soon as you start pulling the bucket out of the water, you notice that your bucket is still empty. No matter how hard you try, you cannot fill your bucket. It is not that you are not capable enough to fill the bucket. No matter how capable or strong you are, you cannot fill it. Alexander was strong. Steve Jobs was capable as well. Both got the same lessons when they were near their deathbed.

We run after money, position, reputation and what not. Though we feel that our bucket is filled, sooner or later we realize that all that effort was useless. Alexander had everything – big palace, money, woman, comfort. His bucket was decorated with diamonds and gold but bottom was still missing. A person who looked from a distance will never know that Alexander's bucket was as useless as a bucket of a poor man.

When the bottom of the bucket called 'DESIRE' is not there, how can you ever fill it? This is what happens when we try to fulfill one desire. As soon as our desire is filled, we realize that the happiness was momentarily. For such a momentary happiness, we traded many years of our life. A poor man also leaves unfulfilled as do the rich. Alexander died equally dissatisfied like a beggar on the street. Both leave empty handed as desires and lust cannot fulfill anyone.

It is no coincidence that in ancient India many kings and princes achieved enlightenment. When you have everything you desire, you can understand and realize its uselessness. Buddha was a prince, Asoka was a king, and Janak was a king. A poor can hardly become enlightened. He is too worried to put a square meal on his plate. When you are hungry, concept of God doesn't make sense. Someone who has never entered the life filled with desires, someone who has never looked carefully at the traps of desires can never understand all this.

Understand your Senses

Once upon a time, there was a king in Japan. He had a very rare breed of goat which he loved very much. He used to feed the goat with the best food but noticed that nothing ever filled its stomach. Whenever something was brought in front of it, it used to start eating. King couldn't understand. He asked his ministers why he was not able to satisfy the hunger of his dear goat. Ministers recommended many ways to satisfy the hunger of the goat, but none worked. King decided to open this challenge to his citizens. He declared that whoever can satisfy the hunger of his goat, will be given lots of gold and land.

Many people came forward and tried. A man came and asked for a time of 5 days for satisfying the goat's hunger. King agreed. The man took the goat to his home and fed the goat with all the best food available in the town. On the 6th morning, he bought the goat back to the king. He said, "I have satisfied the hunger of your goat." King was happy to hear that but ordered a servant to bring some fresh green grass in front of the goat to verify if the goat was really satisfied. As soon as the goat saw the fresh green grass, it started eating it. King got furious and said, "You lied to me. My goat is still not satisfied. What did you feed it? Look how hungry it is."

Like this many men came and claimed to satisfy the hunger of the goat but none could pass the test of fresh green grass. Meanwhile, the goat was getting heavier.

One day a very clever teacher came to the palace. He said that he would need only 3 days to satisfy the hunger of the goat. King was already frustrated with so many false attempts that he exclaimed, "Fair enough! But in case you are not able to do it, I will cut your head off." The teacher agreed and took the goat to his home. He put a plate of grass in front of the goat. As soon as the goat was about to eat it, he hit the goat hard with a stick. The goat didn't understand what happened. It again tried to eat and got another hard hit with the stick. The goat ran away. After 2 hours again the same steps were repeated. The goat was hit every time it moved towards the food.

The teacher presented the goat to the king on the 4th day and said that he has satisfied the hunger of the goat. King looked at the goat. King asked, "Why is my goat looking a little weak? What did you feed it?" The teacher replied, "I fed it with the best ingredients from my kitchen. That helped the goat to lose the unnecessary weight as well. Now you have a fit goat."

King repeated the same experiment. A bowl of grass was brought in front of the goat. As soon as the goat saw the grass, it ran away. King was happy to see this. He said, "You are a truly intelligent man. You have satisfied the hunger of my dear goat."

The teacher walked away with lots of wealth.

You might be laughing at the foolishness of the king but that is how most kings were. But the crux of the matter is that we can never satisfy our sense organs. A tongue can never be satisfied. It will momentarily give you an impression that it is getting satisfied but as soon as the stomach is empty, it is ready. Sometimes it is ready even before that. All our taste sensors are only on the tongue and the tongue cares not of what happens to the rest of the body.

Now we have a new breed of people who call themselves - Foodies. We have people who are servants to their sense of taste. They travel to places in search for the flavours. We eat too much of all kind of stupid foods and then torture ourselves in the gym. Can you ever satisfy your tongue? How many movies can you watch? How many songs can you hear? You cannot satisfy any of the senses.

All our 5 sense organs are designed as a survival mechanism. The five senses are sight, smell, hearing, taste, and touch. The organs that aid in sensing are the eyes, nose, ears, tongue, and skin. The eyes allow us to see what is nearby, judge depth, interpret information, and see color. Nose allows us to smell particles in the air and identify danger and food.

There is nothing special about humans in this respect. Each and every organism on this planet has the sense organs. Some animals or birds even have more advanced sense organs than humans. What is the use of these sense organs? They are simply a survival mechanism. Without eyes, we might not have been able to survive. Without ears and nose, we might end up closer to danger. A tongue helps us to avoid eating anything harmful or poisonous. Skin is an alarm for our body to protect us from anything harmful.

As you can understand, these senses are survival mechanisms, nothing more. But what is happening in our world? We are giving undue importance to survival organs.

In quest of sight, we are doing so many things. The tourism industry is running purely on the sense of sight. We are spending billions of dollars to see the world. For momentary pleasures of sight, we are putting so much effort. We go around seeing mountains, ruins of palaces, tombstones, heritages. What is the use of all these? What can be gained by seeing the history? Remember your last trip. How has it changed/stopped your mind? Are you still the same person or anything has changed about you?

If anything would have really changed, we would have stopped. As soon as we reach home after the trip, we start planning for the next. All the efforts done to satisfy sense organs will only give momentary satisfaction.

Bhagwat Gita says that the human body is like a chariot. The horses on the chariot are senses. The sarathi (charioteer) is the one who has the reins of the horses. The charioteer of our body is our mind. An untamed mind will let the horses (senses) run towards their object of interest. Unless you can bring the mind under your control, it will continue to run wild. Unless you realize the uselessness of following the senses, it will continue to be your master. Unless you achieve a state of no-mind, your mind will keep distracting you. An untamed charioteer can never be a good help.

Another bad news is that senses are all outward bound. People driven by mind will go around the world to satisfy their senses. We watch others; we never bother to watch ourselves. Everybody is watching – what other person is doing, what other person is wearing, how he looks, how others behave…Everybody is watching; watching is not something newly introduced in our life. We watch everybody except ourselves; hence we know more about others than about ourselves. We know nothing about ourselves. We never even witness the functioning of our own mind.

When we go to interviews, we have to prepare about our own positives and negatives. We don't know about ourselves. If someone asks you to describe the negatives of our neighbours or our bosses, we would have so much to speak. Isn't it?

Problems with Expectations

Keeping expectations from others in *not* natural and often reasons of conflicts. Divorce, breakups, and resignations happen because the other person didn't fulfill your expectations. Isn't it? There is something wrong with *expecting* from others. So, what is the problem? When we expect something from others, we keep expectations from our perspective and capability. We don't see other's capacity. Suppose you invite a friend to your house. You love cooking and you decide to impress your guests. You took complete afternoon to learn and cook new dishes, opened new crockery. You all have a great time.

Next week, you were invited by your friend to their house. Now your friend not being a food enthusiast, decide to prepare normal everyday food. You get there and find the arrangement not up to the mark. You start remembering I did that, I did this and they not even did this. You start comparing them with your capacity and interest.

Next time if your friend comes to your place, how will you treat them? What will you cook?

This is the problem why our relationships are straining. We are expecting similar values from another soul, which might be carrying completely different values. In this process even we lose our beautiful values. Because we didn't get the similar treatment from another soul, we lose our values too. Expectations are harmful for us. Lesser the expectations you have from others, the happier you are. Your relationship with others will be better... You shift from expectation to acceptance. Everybody acts based on their capacity and conditioning. We can do based on our capacity. What we have does not necessarily be present in others. Don't have expectations because everybody has a unique mind. No mind can ever be the same.

Emotion is a word with deep meaning. If you look closely emotion has the word motion in it. So basically anything which causes motion in you is called emotion. When we are angry, we start throwing things. When we are angry, we throw our hand on others. When you get the emotion of anger, your breathing will suddenly change. Your breathing will become irritated and chaotic. A trembling will get into your breathing. Your whole body will like to do something, shatter something, throw something, only then you feel little relaxation. Your blood pressure change, your heart starts moving faster. Certain hormones are released in the blood. Just a few thoughts of anger can cause so much motion inside your body.

Emotions are the results of what you are thinking. Fear and Anger are some of the most dominant emotions among the present generation. You are responsible for the way you are now. Resentment, anger, jealousy, pain, & hurt are the poison that you drink but expect someone else to die. When fear is there love cannot be present. Isn't it? Fear and love are diagonally opposite emotions. You cannot love and fear the same thing. If you love God, there is no fear. If you fear God, there cannot be any love.

Every organism fears. Some might fear for their life. Only human has the capability to fear without even a clear physical danger. Why? Because we can imagine.

"Fear is when you are not living with life you are living in your mind," says Sadhguru. "Your fear is often what will happen next. This means that our fear is always about the thing which doesn't exist. If your fear is about the non-existent, your fear is absolutely imaginary. If you are suffering the non-existential, we call this insanity." It is not surprising that many people who feel directionless in their life, develop fear. Fear of the unknown is stupidity.

We are creating fear in our minds and thoughts. I heard one talk of Will Smith, famous Hollywood actor on fear. He said that he and some of his friends were in Dubai and one of his friend suggested to go for skydiving the next day and they all agreed. But later during the night, he was really fearful. The fear was so intense that he couldn't sleep properly. He said that it's not the fear of jumping (skydiving) from a plane which panics people but the waiting to jump that gets the fellow. We constantly imagine a night before our jump for all the bad things that could happen. We feel that sinking feeling in our solar plexus. The more we think about the fear, the stronger it gets. We start to reason ourselves out of the situation. We start planning maybe I will call in sick tomorrow and avoid this all together. In fact, Will tells his own example where he couldn't sleep a night before the actual jump. When he did jump out of the plane he said, "In one second you realize that it is the most blissful experience of your life. You are flying. You realize at the point of maximum danger there is zero fear. It's Bliss! The lesson for me was: why were you scared in the bed the night before? Why do you need that fear for? Why would you need enjoy the breakfast? Fear of what? You are nowhere near the airplane."

You can understand that your fear was just negative thoughts. The thought that you might die or feel terrible when you jump caused you so much trouble. You couldn't sleep properly, eat properly. It just ruins your day.

Fear is like salt in our food. If it is less or more, life becomes difficult. We should be concerned about too much salt. Too much fear hampers our growth as a full-blown personality. It's like putting a plant in the ground and then putting too many restrictions for it to grow. The tree will find its way but it will not be the same if it got a chance to grow freely and fully. Fear is not a bad feeling but taking it to your mind and making porridge out of it is. Fear of spiders, snakes or insects is not natural. None of the fear is natural. Remember in your childhood you feared ghosts under your bed or in dark rooms. There was no ghost. You imagined it (information drove that imagination).

That is the main problem with us. We are creating fear in our minds and thoughts.

Famous comedian and actor Jim Carrey said, "So many of us choose our path out of fear disguised as practicality." So true, isn't it? We make most of our decisions out of fear. We chose our college majors based not on what we love but what will give us a stable career. We choose our career, out of fear (what will happen if I fail in my passion). In fact Jim

Carrey added, "My father could have been a great comedian but he didn't believe that was possible for him. So he made a conservative choice. Instead, he got a safe job as an accountant and when I was 12 years old, he was let go from that safe job and our family had to do whatever we could to survive. I learned many great lessons from my father. Not the least of which was that you can fail at what you don't want, so you might as well take a chance on doing what you love."

When you start having fearful thoughts you give more energy to your fear. To cut the cord between the emotion and thought is to give awareness and acceptance to it. This is who you are. You might have to do it frequently. You cannot get rid of it. You have to accept it. When you truly focus on it, it transforms. Only human being has the capability to really look deep into the emotions we have.

Anger is another highly negative emotion. Anger has many forms. It can be subtle, just in the mind, it could be in the form of irritation, it could be in the form of loud words, and sometimes it can come out in actions. From a Buddhist perspective, anger is a potentially destructive emotion often related to greediness and attachment. While anger can be a source of holy wisdom when it brings awareness, it has the potential to descend into hatred or aggression. How does anger create? It all starts with a thought. Suppose someone comes to you and start talking rudely to you. What will happen? Let me take it really slow for you to understand. The words from the person's mouth will fall on your ears. Your brain will interpret the meaning of those words. A thought will be generated. Thought might be - How can he say something like that? How dare he?. Further thoughts can be - Let me counterattack him by saying something. You will generate another thought on what to speak. You can become aggressive based on your impulses and tendencies. Now in real life all this happens fast, as if it is happens automatically. But if you are aware, you can see what thoughts are getting generated. Action or emotion is just a byproduct of what you were thinking. You have no control over your thoughts. Your mind has stopped taking instructions from you.

The point of anger is rooted in your false perception that you can change the situation by losing your temper with it. You only mess up the situation by being angry. Besides there is substantial medical and scientific evidence that in a state of anger, you are literally poisoning your system. Your cells love cells of others. When you hate another cellular body, your cells become confused. Why does this guy hate another organism? We are all the same. They become confused and, in that confusion, they start harming themselves. Cancer is one of the primary outcomes of such negative emotions. When we remain negative for a large period, the toxins in our body increases and leads to many diseases. So next time you are angry, know that you are going to harm only yourself.

Everything around us is pure energy. Our brain is like translators which help us interpret these frequencies and help us with our perceived physical reality. While all such vibrations take a physical form, there are non-physical energies as well. Perfect example is our Thoughts. Our thoughts are just different kind of vibrations. Like every different atom have different vibrations, our thoughts too carry different vibrations depending upon the kind of thought. If you are thinking about a positive thought and that in turns make you feel happy, it's vibrating at a higher frequency. If a thought is negative, it is vibrating at a lower frequency. For example, "I have no money" has a much lower frequency than "I have vast amounts of money."

Whenever you get angry, you get into lower state of vibration. Your vibration not only penetrate your body and but also everything on this planet. Your mind is not only letting down the soul but also the soul of another person you are angry at. Have you noticed we start shaking in the fit of anger?

Anger brings delusion and attachment. You shout at somebody or frown at someone; you cannot get over them quickly. The incidence just sticks to your mind. Your mind will replay that incidence again and again. The incidence lingers on.

Sadly, In our present world we have equated anger with power. Aggression is power. We even have superheroes that become powerful by just getting angry. But is it really a powerful feeling? Do you feel weak or powerful when you are angry? When I lose control of myself, when my words are not what they should be. When I have to regret my words and actions, even apologize by saying: 'Sorry, I didn't mean to say all that, it just happened in the heat of the moment', it cannot be power. We often hear criminals pleading innocence by saying that: "It just happened in the heat of the moment. I didn't want to kill him."

When all this is happening, anger cannot be a powerful feeling. Anger makes the soul weak. You lose your peace and physical health. When you say: "I didn't mean to say that", it clearly means you were not yourself in that moment of anger. Who were you then? You were the slave of your tendencies, your sanskaras and your own mind. You lost the awareness of what to say and what not to say. When we are angry, we try to cause harm to others. But as time passes by, we realize that we have caused more harm to ourselves.

Do you know we chose anger? We are unconsciously choosing when, where, with whom, how much and for how long. Do you react the same way if a junior and a senior use the same words?

Once there was a monk in a monastery. He would often complain that he didn't get proper peace within the monastery during his meditation. One day the monk decided to meditate alone. He took a boat out to the middle of the lake, dropped his anchor, closed his eyes and began his meditation. After a few minutes of undisturbed silence, he suddenly feels a bump of another boat colliding with his own. With his eyes closed he sensed anger rising within him. He could notice this own thought, "can't the other boatman see that someone is meditating here? He must be a reckless and insensitive fellow!" He kept his eyes closed. He feels the bump again, though this time it was gentler. Unable to control his rage he opens his eyes, ready to scream at the boatman who dared to disturb him. To his surprise it was an empty boat that has probably got untethered and floated to the middle of the lake.

At that moment the monk got a realization. The anger was always inside him. All he needed was an outside bump to bring it outside him. From then on whenever he came across someone who irritated him or provoked him to anger, he reminded himself: "The other person is merely an empty boat. The anger is within me."

This is a great story for all of us. Let us take responsibility of our own anger and remind ourselves that anger is inside of me and I have a choice to not let that anger out of me. Anger is like a plant in our garden. The more you cultivate it, the stronger it grows. The more we use anger in our day to day situation, angrier we get.

It is not necessary that we react to everything. Step back and ask yourself if the matter is really worth responding to?

Desire and expectation leads to anger. We expect people to behave in a particular way with us. When that doesn't happen, we feel that we have the right to get angry.

In case you were wrong, the anger sooner or later converts to regret. Regret brings more attachment. By regretting you don't move away from the person or situation, you move more into it. Have you ever observed that whoever you are angry with or hate, you think of that person more than yourself?

11. Think before you ACT

We have often heard the old adage "Think before you act". Still, we are not able to act in the exact same way we want. Why is there always a gap? I don't want to get angry but still, i get angry. I don't want to eat junk food but i still end up eating them. Why there is a constant gap between what we think and how we act?

Now, this happens to me all the time. I have to give a presentation and i am all ready. I have rehearsed what i will speak. But what happens during the presentation? Do you speak what you have planned? Did you speak what you plan or something else? One that we prepare and one we speak is quite different. Isn't it? And then there is a third version which happens when we are coming back after the presentation and we think, "Oh! I could have said that." or "Oh! I completely missed telling the audience that point."

Why do we act in a different way? We make New Year resolutions and then the very next morning, decide to postpone them. Who made the plans and who failed to execute? If you have been a little aware, above phenomenon must have been already noticed in your life as well.

From just the above three paragraphs, isn't it a little clear that action is not completely in our hands? We want to act how a robot acts but sadly we are not able to act like that. Do we really have control over our actions?

What happens when you want to get a glass of water?

Step 1: Your body tells you that it is thirsty.

Step 2: You will impulsively think whether to go right away or wait to drink water

Step 3: Once you decide to go, your body will automatically move. Your feet will automatically move to the place where water is. There is no awareness required here. It is full robotic motion. You are working as a pre-programmed machine.

Step 4: You drink water and come back.

Your bodily action is completely pre-programmed. Look at all the people on the road. They are walking like robots. Their awareness is not on the road. Now, look at a child who is learning to walk. Look how aware the kid is. Once programmed, we can do any activity without any awareness. We can swim, walk, eat, and read without any attention to the act. Action happens automatically.

"What great things would you attempt if you knew you could not fail?" - Robert H. Schuller

Beliefs and our conditioning also greatly impact our actions. Sadly, most of us don't even realize that. Say, you are meeting someone you really love and admire. Do you have to think about how to behave in front of them? You automatically do and act as per your beliefs and thoughts about that person. You don't have any control over your words or actions.

What happens when you meet someone you hate? Do you have to ponder what would be your words and action towards that person? No. We act based on our thought impulses. Although we want to believe that we perform an action but actions are not in our control. Based on the discussion so far, we can understand that actions are a byproduct of something and might not be always in our control – just like our thoughts!

Like we have programmed our body for all the bodily actions, our mental actions are also pre-programmed. While we can learn the body actions on our own, society plays a vital role in shaping our mental actions.

A kid raised in a terrorist's family will be fed with so much hate that by the time he becomes 7 or 8, he will flaunt guns and speak the language of terror. All his subsequent actions will be automatically happening through the pre-programmed mind. He will fight for his religious beliefs. He will be ready to kill and die for his conditioning.

Mental actions determine our life. Isn't it? Once our minds are programmed, it is almost impossible to think fresh. If you look at the terror camps, the training begins when a boy is very young. It is very easy to program someone that young. You can easily put venom and hatred into the mind of a 5-year-old. There is no resistance in a young mind. I often see people debating on social media, cafeterias and news channels about topics ranging from political to religious.

Have you ever seen any party convinced by other party's arguments? Have you truly convinced another person? It will never happen. In fact, you will notice that the other party will become more adamant with their original thoughts and opinions. They might even become aggressive during their debates. We as minds don't like our beliefs and ideas being taken down and murdered. We fight and act based on our minds.

Thinking before acting is very difficult because of the reason that we act mostly in a pre-programmed way. We get angry and then after some time think, "Oh! I should have not said that" or "Oh! Why did I react like that?" And then comes the usual drama or regret. Regret is an emotion which will only come when we act in such a pre-programmed way. We regret our action when we didn't think it through.

When you say sorry for your actions, you are indirectly admitting that you didn't mean to do it. It happened in the heat of the moment. Your original programming took over for those split seconds. Once you calmed down, you say 'sorry'. Then what happens? You again become your mind on some other day. You again lose the ability to think. You act without thinking.

We have already seen in earlier chapters that we cannot think anything that we already don't know. The memory and information that we carry is the base of our thinking and arguments.

Bodily actions help us to do very basic activities. Bodily activity is also mostly pre-programmed. We practice a lot. Army trains fiercely. Why? So that when the real fight comes, they don't have to think about it. They can act as they have programmed the body.

Everyone must have heard about the golf ace – Tiger Woods. He said, "I get so entrenched in the moment; I guess my subconscious mind takes over. I don't know what the terminology is but there are many putts and shots where I don't remember anything. I remember seeing the ball fly and remember preparing for the shot, pulling my club out of the bag. Once I am behind the ball, I am walking in the shot, I don't remember until I see the ball leave. It's a weird thing."

John Montague was an American golfer, held by some to be among the greatest golfers in the world during the early 1930s. People claimed that the ball went where Montague wanted it to go. He said, "Golf to me is played with the head, mind or brain or whatever you wish to call it. Of course, there are fundamentals of stance, grip, swing; but I must have a clear, clean mental picture of what I am doing before I play the shot. That mental picture takes charge of the muscular reaction. If there is no mental picture – what happens is a mere guess."

You can see cricketers having lots and lots of training sessions throughout their lives. Even the best in the business have to sweat in the sun, practicing and perfecting that one stroke. Why do you think they are doing that? They are doing that because they want the muscles to move robotically when they are playing a live match. There is rarely time to think. The reason why tailenders are not able to play the ball well has to do with this practice. They are trained to bowl. If you are not trained, you cannot move your hands and legs in such a small duration.

When you see a batsman play an effortless stroke, you can be 100% sure that he has played that stroke in nets at least a thousand times. His hands and legs move automatically in the direction of the ball. There is little thinking involved. The hand-eye coordination builds almost like a circuit in the brain.

The mind automatically controls our day to day actions.

Throughout our lives, we keep focussing on the actions without thinking about the source of those actions. We focus on the outcome, but never on the source. We tell our children not to steal (action). We tell the children not to lie (action). We tell the children to study hard (action). We tell children what should be the outcome. Not speaking a lie is an outcome and not the source. Speaking a lie or a truth is dependent on some factors. If i am born and raised in an environment where lies, deceit are common, i as a child will learn and exhibit the same behaviour. Is it not? Telling a child not to lie would be foolish in such a scenario.

Make sure the child doesn't have any influence of people telling lies around him. Kids mimic the world they see. If you want your children to change, you have to change first. You cannot lie to your spouse and ask your children to always speak the truth. If you fight with your spouse at the home, expect that your children will also learn to fight and disagree with their colleagues in schools.

There is an interesting story of King Vikramaditya and ghost Betal. Vikramaditya was a legendary emperor of ancient India. Often characterized as an ideal king, he was known for his intelligence, generosity, courage, and patronage for scholars. Every day the king used to arrange a morning assembly to meet his people and know their problems.

One day during the morning assembly a tantric (person involved in occult activities) came to the king and gifted him a fruit. The tantric didn't say anything and disappeared in the crowd. This started happening daily. The king was surprised at the reason why this tantric is giving him a fruit daily - what can be the purpose!

One day after the morning assembly, Vikramaditya decided to break open the fruit. To his astonishment, he saw precious pearls and diamonds inside it. Vikramaditya ordered for cutting off all the previous days' fruits and found valuable pearls and diamonds in all. King was really confused.

Next morning the tantric again came to see the king. King asked him, "Are you trying to lure a king by giving him expensive jewels. What is the purpose of all this? What favours do you want by showing such magic tricks?

Tantric said, "I have not come to meet the king. I have come to meet the man called Vikramaditya. I have heard about his intelligence and valour. For enhancing my spiritual and occult powers, I am doing a yagya (fire sacrifice) inside a cave in the nearby jungle and I want a favour from him."

King asked, "What kind of favour? It will be an honour for me if i can help a person attain a spiritual goal."

Tantric kept a strange condition for the king. He said, "I need your time tonight. I want you to come all alone to the cave in the nearby jungle. I have heard about your intelligence, valour, and courage and i know only you can help me. But you must come alone."

Even the kings are hungry for appreciation. Although the ministers warned the king, Vikramaditya agreed.

That night around midnight Vikramaditya reached the cave. The tantric was performing a fire sacrifice and chanting mantras. Vikramaditya greeted the tantric and asked the purpose of this meeting. Tantric was happy that the king stood by his words. He said, "I am happy to see that you have come on time. I have a very strange task for you. Head north of this place. You will find a dense jungle after a few miles. When you cross that, you will find a cremation ground. In the middle of the crematorium, you will find a tree. On that tree, you will find a dead body hanging upside down. Your only job is to bring that dead body to me before dawn."

Vikram asked, "That is a really strange request. What will you do with the dead body?"

Tantric got annoyed. He said, "Do as i say. You have promised to follow my orders. Go and bring the dead body."

Vikram agreed to go in the direction advised by the tantric. Tantric said, "Remember not be speak and you will be alright."

Vikramaditya got confused - what is this strange condition. Nothing of this night was making any sense to him. As promised he set out into the jungle. It was a no moon night and the jungle was infested with snakes and wild animals. Soon the king reached the cremation ground. He noticed a dead tree in the middle. When he came closer, he noticed a dead body hanging upside down on a branch. He climbed the tree and pushed the body down.

Suddenly the dead body started laughing. Vikram must have been really terrified. This was no dead body. This was a ghost.

This was the ghost of Betal. Vikramaditya overpowered the ghost and put it on his back and started on his journey back to the cave where the tantric was performing the yagya. Ghost started talking to Betal. Betal said, "Vikram i knew you will come one day. That cunning tantric will definitely send you. I knew it. You are very powerful. Whatever i have heard about you is right."

Since the tantric told Vikramaditya to be quiet, he remained silent. Betal said, "I know you will not speak a word. If you speak, i will fly away back to that tree. Not even a single word should come from your mouth."

Vikramaditya was navigating his way through the dense dark jungle. Imagine the amount of fear that Vikramaditya must be going through. Dark night, wild animals, snakes crawling nearby, ghost on the back and to top it all, he cannot say a word. When we are afraid, whistling or even talking to ourselves alleviates the fear. With complete silence, fear also magnifies.

Betal said, "Since the way is long and you will not speak, why not i tell you a story. This will also help us pass our time."

Poor King! He couldn't even say no. If he said no, Betal would fly away. He had to play in the hands of that ghost. Betal started narrating a story. It was an interesting one. King's mind also got attracted to the plot.

The world loves fiction novels. We love fantasy and sci-fi movies and serials. Is it not? Fiction helps us forget our miserable life. It takes us to an imaginary world of superheroes, giant monsters and what not.

King's mind was stuck in the interesting plot. He was listening to the story carefully and also constantly contemplating the right or the wrong. When the story reached the climax, Betal asked, "O king! You are known for your intelligence and wisdom. Tell me what should be the proper ending to this story. Do the justice."

Vikramaditya was already into the story. He was finding pleasure in the story. He was already contemplating. Sadly he cannot speak else the ghost of Betal will fly away. He kept silent.

Betal said, "I admire your control and patience. But remember that in case you know the answer and still don't speak, your head will burst into 100 pieces. If you don't know the answer then i will remain in your captivity."

King was now in a dilemma. He couldn't speak but he knew the answer in his head. He couldn't control his mind. He spoke and gave the verdict. Betal said, "King you are very intelligent. You have done justice. But now that you have spoken, i will have to fly back." Betal flew away. King followed him.

This happened 25 times that night. Each time Vikram captured Betal, it would tell a story that ended with a riddle. If Vikram doesn't know the answer to the question, the ghost consented to remain in his captivity. If the king knows the answer but still keeps quiet, then his head shall burst into hundred pieces.

It took 25 such efforts prior to which the king got rid of his mind. Vikram was strong and courageous but his mind was weak. His mind was not under his control. Even if he wanted not to think, he had no control. It took him 25 such trips before he could silence his mind. After the 25th Story, the king was silent. King was not contemplating or thinking. Betal was impressed.

Betal told the truth about the tantric. Betal also revealed that tantric's plan is to sacrifice Vikram, beheading him as he bowed in front of the goddess. Then tantric could gain control over the Betal and sacrifice his soul, thus achieving his evil ambition. The Betal suggested that the king should ask the tantric how to perform his obeisance, and then take advantage of that moment to behead the sorcerer himself. Vikramaditya does exactly as told by Betal and he was blessed by the Gods.

There was a reason why Betal didn't tell the story of the evil tantric in the very first trip. He waited till 25th story to finally reveal the evil plot of the tantric. Betal saw some spark in the king. He knew that the king can be a great ruler of men. He realized that the Vikram was under a commitment and would try to obey the tantric. He was the man of his words. As long as the mind is there, he cannot argue with such a commitment. Vikram would have dismissed to act as per Betal. A mind acts as per its belief and conditioning.

A person with no-mind can be argued with.

So what does this story teaches us? Go beyond your mind. The mind is stopping us from liberation and freedom. The mind will keep you occupied with useless things. Materialism, communism, fascism are all inventions of the mind. A mind is stopping us. Unless we go beyond our mind, we cannot control any of our actions. We will continue to act like a robot.

12. You cannot leave your mind

Once upon a time there lived an old saint. His tattered hut was located outside a town on the road side. One day while the saint was sitting outside his house, a horse approached near him. The equestrian greeted the saint and said, "I have come from a distant town and i am planning to settle in this town. Can you tell me how the people of this town are?"

Saint looked up carefully and thought for a second. He said, "Before i answer that question i want to know how the people from where you are coming from were." The man said, "Why do you want to know that? I am asking you a simple question and you are making it complicated."

Saint said, "I need to know the answer to my question before i can comment anything."

Horse rider said, "If you insist, the people of my last village were terrible. They are the reason why i have left that village and decided to settle elsewhere. Even remembering their name fills my heart with hatred."

Saint said, "Well my friend i must warn you now. People of this village are even worse. They will not let you survive. I think you should go to some other village."

Believing the saint, the horse rider went in a different direction.

Few days passed by. One day a bullock cart stopped in front of the saint's hut. A family was riding it will lots of luggage. Saint understood that these people have come to relocate to his village. The family again asked the same question, "How are the people in this village?"

Saint said, "Why don't you tell me about the people from the village where you are coming from?"

The man said, "Oh! They were wonderful. Our heart was filled with sorrow when we had to decide to leave them behind."

Saint said, "Well! You will be amazed that the people in this village are equally good. They are very caring and humble. You should make this your new home."

Why did the saint give different reply to two different persons asking the same question?

You can leave the village or your home but you cannot leave your mind behind. The mind will go with you wherever you go. Even if you decide to leave everything and go to Himalayas, your mind will accompany you. It cannot be left behind. Wherever you go, your mind will create the same kind of world around you.

If you really want to change your world, you cannot achieve that with your mind. Mind is past. It cannot create anything new. Mind is ego. Mind is memory. Mind is "I". Mind is what you really are. If you are not able to gel with the people in one town, there is great chance that you will have friction at other places as well. Your idiosyncrasies will be with you. You have to leave your past behind. You have to leave your mind behind.

In the East, it was society's duty to feed their saints. Buddha used to carry a begging bowl where he went. People who have conquered their mind and senses were considered supreme. They don't need to work to earn bread. They don't need to build a hut to sleep. People would open their houses, wherever they went. It was the responsibility of the society to take care of their enlightened ones. No one would ask spiritual gurus to do something creative or do some work. Work is for the people with mind. Very few dared to look beyond the mind.

Lot of writers will suggest controlling your mind and thoughts. Well we all have tried that out. It doesn't work. How many times we tried to sleep but our thoughts kept us awake? How many times we tried not to get angry and then one day we lost our cool? It's almost impossible to control our thoughts. We are the thoughts. Our thoughts are not different from who we are. Who will control who? There are is no duality. It's just one part of mind trying to control another part. Mind gives us an impression of duality. You might have noticed yourself or others talking while alone. Who are you talking to?

It is very easy to fall in the traps of the mind. In India, we call the world "Moh Maya" which means the world is combination of desire and illusion. Why do we say so? Because whatever we see in this world which has any human mind behind it, is an illusion of the mind. They don't mean that the mountains and rivers are illusion. Earth is real. Mind creates desires and illusions.

What is an illusion? Dictionary meaning of illusion is "an instance of a wrong or misinterpreted perception of a sensory experience". Illusion is anything which appears to be there but it is not there. Anything which is not permanent is an illusion. Look around your world. Everything will be taken away from you one fine day. Your death is not an illusion.

Mind gives duality. If you reach a state of no-mind, who will you talk to? You can be silent. You can be finally at peace. You can finally be happy. Notice that when you are very happy, there is no mind. That is the reason why we say that don't make any promise when you are very happy. We are not thinking at all while we are happy. We are just simply in the moment, totally. Try to think next time you are smiling due to happiness.

When Buddha left his home in search for the meaning of life, he didn't leave his mind behind. He went from one guru to another. He tried to torture his body by fasting, standing on one leg and what not. He did whatever he was told but he was still not getting what he was looking for. In desperation, he just let go one day. In that let go, he attained realization. Letting go everything of the mind brings you to meditation. Desire to achieve enlightenment is also a barrier. The desire belongs to the mind. When we just let go of every desire, we have a chance to see beyond mind.

Bucket list is of the mind. What do you really achieve by jumping of a plane? What did you really achieve by scuba diving? What you get climbing Himalayas? What did Alexander achieve on his conquest of the world? There is no achievement. May be you will get few Facebook likes and comments. Those mean nothing as well. Bucket lists are designed for the mind. They might be designed by some clever marketing company - probably a tourism company. We spend thousands of dollars to complete our bucket list. I don't even want to talk about the struggle to earn that money in the first place.

Self means silence

When Jesus was asked to prove "Are you the son of God", he kept silent. That was the wisest thing to do. When you are demanded proof of something which is beyond proof, the remedy is silence. You are telling someone you have a pain in your leg, and they ask you, "Come on, prove it to me, how do I believe you?" How can you prove your pain?

Silence has always been within us. It is not accumulation. There is so much physical activity which is going on right now in your body. Blood is circulating, oxygen is getting exchanged, digestion is happening. Your heart is constantly beating. Your lungs are expanding and contracting. This is just a miniscule activity compared to the movements happening inside our body right at this moment. All our trillions of cells are doing different activity constantly to keep us alive. We are like a planet to these 100 trillion cells.

Do you hear any noise? Listen closely. You only hear your heartbeat when you are scared or after you run a quick sprint. So much activity is going on but with pin drop silence.

When a baby is formed inside a mother's body, it experiences only silence. There is no word. It is in eternal silence for 9 months. There is complete darkness inside. Not a single source of light.

From that silence, a baby is born. Silence is our mother and our very source. Once we come to this world, we are constantly bombarded by sounds. Everyone is ready to teach something to a baby. Somebody teaches him to say "Papa" or "mama", while others want them to say something else. A child is constantly bombarded with noise. We try teaching them language. We give them information - alphabets, numbers and what not.

There is a constant noise we face. This noise is the beginning of a mind. Information, memory, experiences all form the basis of the mind and thoughts. Mind means words. Is it anything else? Can you think without words? Once the mind is set up, it cannot stop chattering. It has so many topics to speak about. It has an opinion about everything.

Before the mind is formed, we have innocence. Look at all the kids below age 2 years. They are bundles of joy. There is no mind working in the background. They are smiling, jumping around all day long. The energy is so much that we cannot even fathom. Why?

There is no mind. Mind gives you a long face. When there is no mind, you are just enjoying. You are totally in the moment. There might be noise outside, but inside there is silence, there is peace.

Our whole education is for the mind, by the mind, and of the mind. Our desires and ambitions can only be fulfilled by the mind. Mind pushes you to become somebody.

The absence of mind brings joy and smile. At the moment when you are truly ecstatic, there is no mind. We generally do all the stupid things when we are super happy. We overcommit, overpromise. We become a kind person. There is no mind. That is a different story that after we come back to our normal state, we regret. The mind is back!

The mind can never stop chattering. The mind is confusion. You cannot achieve peace of mind. This phrase "peace of mind" is not feasible. A mind is synonymous to the storm in the ocean. Once the storm is no more, the ocean is peaceful. We never say peaceful storm. Storm simply isn't there anymore. Imagine that there is a storm in the ocean and there are big waves. If you are on a ship, you will be panicking. Your ship will be swinging left to right.

Now imagine that there is a storm in the ocean and you are 50 feet inside the water. You are watching the storm but are separated from it. The storm cannot affect you. Fighting the storm is not a wise decision. Storms will blow your sails apart. Similarly, there is no point of fighting the mind. You can never win.

You have lived in a certain way up to now – don't you want to live in a different way? You think in a certain way up to now – don't you want to think in a different way?

A mind is noise. You have to separate yourself from the mind. You have to forget your past, prejudices, and stereotypes to truly live peacefully. A mind is past. A mind is a graveyard. Your past is always influencing your present. If you see a sunset and you exclaim, "Wow! This is so beautiful", you have lost the sunset. The moment you judge anything, you have already used the mind. Is it not? How else will you know if this is beautiful or not? Show the same sunset to a 1-year-old and observe what he or she does. The kid will simply observe. There is no judgement there. The kid is really enjoying the sunset.

Judging anything requires a mind. Even you said the above words nonverbally, it is still your mind speaking. Once the mind takes over, you have lost the present moment. The present moment is gone. Remember the age-old adage – "Live in the present moment"? This cannot be followed by people who live in the mind. How can past (mind) and present (no-mind) be present at the same time.

That is why we constantly miss moments. If you can look at a flower, without any judgement, past memories then only you can be total with the flower.

Look around you. Trees are growing in silence. Flowers, birds, animals, moon are growing in silence. There is no noise. There is no ego in nature. Ego (another dimension of mind) makes noise. Go out sometime during the late night and listen to the quietness.

A mind doesn't even let us be silent while we retire to bed. A mind is constantly working in the background. We call such activity as dreams. Sleep with lots of dreams is not a great sleep. Dreamless sleep is the best sleep. Power naps are the best sleep if there is no dream. Without dreams, we feel energetic even after a short nap. If there were a lot of dreams, even an 8- hour sleep, is not sufficient.

Return back to silence, drop all your past, experiences. Once you drop all your past, what will you think about!

Think about it!

It is said that when Buddha attained enlightenment, he went silent. There was nothing to speak. The followers who were following him for years were shocked. They were expecting that once their master attains the highest, they will also get the benefit of that knowledge. Buddha remained silent. Mythology says that all the angels in the heaven got frightened and said, "Once in a millennium someone blossoms so fully like Buddha. Now he is silent, is not saying a word!" It is said all the angels approached Buddha and asked him to say something, please speak something.

Buddha said, "Those who know, they know, even without my saying, and those who do not know, they will not know by my words. Any description of life to a blind man is of no use. One who has not tasted the ambrosia of existence, of life, no point in talking to them about it? So I am silent," he said. How can you convey something so intimate, something so personal? Words cannot. And many scriptures in the past have declared, "Words end where truth begins." The argument was very good.

Meditation and Yoga are ancient practices to attain silence. They are designed to take us beyond the mind.

You must have realized that it is very difficult to be silent. The mind will not let you sit silently in meditation. As soon as you sit down and close your eyes, the mind will start to play around. When you are not doing anything, the mind is free. When you are sleeping, the mind is free. While you are awake and doing something, you can suppress the mind. When in sleep, that repression is also lifted. That is why we get such weird dreams sometimes. Mind is playing around while you are asleep.

Confucius says," Silence is a true friend who never betrays."

Silence is your real nature. A mind is given to you by society. It is similar to your name. Your name is given to you by your family, which are not you. Similarly, the mind is not you. It is your conditioning since childhood. Your original nature was silence. You were born from silence.

You have to go back to your original nature for real peace and happiness. Meditation is only possible in silence. Mind and meditation cannot coexist. Silence and noise cannot exist together.

13. Poverty cannot lead you inside

Once there was a rich man who fell very sick. Doctors examining him gave him only a few days to live. Many guests arrived to see the great man before he passed away. One of the guests asked him, "You must be dying as a very satisfied man. You are leaving behind an empire of 10 billion dollars." The dying replied, "I wish. My goal was 100 billion dollars. I am dying as a highly unsatisfied man."

Everyone is running after money and fame. There is a race to hoard materials. There is an innate pleasure in material possessions. There is a pleasure in getting recognition from others. People are doing everything possible to get moments of fame and recognition. Becoming a top cricketer, actor or singer is difficult, but if you are desperate for fame at any cost, killing is an easy way to make to the newspaper headlines. History is filled with examples of people who have killed, just to become famous. Daniel Gonzalez, Dennis Rader, Mijailo Mijailovic, and so many others have resorted to mass killing to seek quick fame and glory.

University of Alabama criminologist Adam Lankford has explained the repetition of such incidents as a product of hunger for status. "Some mass shooters succumb to terrible delusions of grandeur, and seek fame and glory through killing," he wrote.

With social media in full swing, we see people rising to instant fame by doing something unique or sometimes even stupid.

Look at the lives of the great spiritual souls which have walked on the earth. Buddha was born to a king. He had all the luxury that a man can imagine. On Buddha's birth, his father, King Suddhodana called many astrologers to predict his son's future. One of the astrologers predicted that the son of the king would renounce the world and become a great ascetic.

Suddhodana, who was determined that his son should be a great king, confined the prince within the palace and surrounded him with earthly pleasures and luxuries, thereby concealing the realities of life that might encourage him to renounce these pleasures and become an ascetic. Even the dead leaves and flowers in the garden were removed before the dawn so that death in any form should not touch the king.

Buddha's real name was Siddhartha. Siddhartha was given all the luxury and happiness. Even if Siddhartha desired to venture out on the streets of his kingdom, all the poor, old, and diseased were removed from the streets. Old and the poor were ordered by the king to remain in their homes till his son's trip was completed. Streets were filled with happy looking people, dancing women, flowers.

Siddhartha was even married to a beautiful young princess. Buddha's father did everything possible to distract Buddha.

After leading a sheltered existence surrounded by luxury and pleasure in his younger years, Prince Siddhartha ventured out of his palace for the first time without informing his father. He was accompanied by his charioteer. Both sneaked out of the palace gate. On his journey through the streets, first time Siddhartha saw the real world. For the first time, he saw an old man, a sick person, and a dead man.

On seeing a dead man, Siddhartha asked his charioteer, "What has happened to this man? Where is everyone taking him to?"

His charioteer was hesitant, to tell the truth to the prince. On constant insisting by the prince, charioteer told him that this man has died and everybody is taking him to the cremation grounds.

Behind the man was the family of the deceased. Women were crying and there was an atmosphere of extreme sadness. Till then the Buddha was shielded from all sufferings.

The prince was shocked to hear this. He asked, "Will I also die?" Charioteer hesitantly replied, "Yes. Everyone who is born has to become old and die one day. You will also become old and weak and one day leave this body."

A great awareness dawned on Siddhartha. This was the turning point for a to-be king. He realized the irrelevance of the physical world and the material possessions when the goal of this body is death. This was the point when he left all the comforts of a palace and went in the search of the meaning of life.

Mahavir was born in 599 B.C. as a **prince** in Bihar, India. At the age of 30, he left his family and royal household, gave up his worldly possessions, including clothing and become a monk.

King Janak attained enlightenment. Most Jain prophets were kings. Ram was born to a king. In fact, many Hindu avatars were kings or son of kings. Why did Buddha become discontented? Why did he start in search of something meaningful? Wasn't all the luxury meaningful enough? Why would a king abandon his clothes, all the luxury in search of something beyond materialism?

These are some of the questions which we all should ask ourselves.

Most of us, who have never seen that kind of affluence, might not be able to answer these questions. People who have to work day and night to feed their family cannot answer these questions. People who are running after materialistic possessions and goals might find it difficult to answer these questions.

What can be beyond money? Only extremely rich and courageous can answer. Why courageous? Simply because it takes guts to admit that whatever efforts one did to accumulate wealth and fame were useless. Only spiritually evolved persons can understand the fallacy of desires. Most rich will not admit that. They will continue to keep a fake smile in the public to look successful.

Buddha was able to see the irrelevance of luxury and possessions because he was rich. He lived in affluence; he lived in all that which was possible, all comforts, and all material gadgets. Suddenly he becomes aware; he was only twenty-nine when he realized the inner darkness. There was so much light outside, hence it is easy to see inner darkness. Only when there is so much richness outside, a person realizes the inner poverty. Someone who has not seen desires closely cannot see the irrelevance of it.

Buddha abandoned his palace. That's what happened to Mahavir; he also escaped from a palace. This realization can rarely happen to a beggar. He already has no money, for him, money is the ultimate goal. All his life he will run after money and then die empty-handed.

This is a real story. A few years back, a beggar was found dead on one of the streets of my hometown. Since no one was claiming the body, the government municipality came to take the body for cremation. When they searched the pockets of the overcoat worn by the man, they noticed something. There was currency notes of 1000 rupees stacked in one of the pockets. When they continued searching, they were shocked to see more such notes. Sum total of the money with which that beggar died came to around 2, 00,000 rupees!

It turned out that this beggar after the day's end would go to a nearby shop and convert all the coins and small denomination notes into bigger currency notes. He was accumulating the money from years. He had so much money, yet he died in such a terrible state. Funny incident happened after that. Some newspapers published this news in the next day print. Many people reached the police station claiming that the deceased was their relative.

It's funny when you realize that money is at the center of every goal. Isn't it? Jim Carrey is a world famous comedian. He once said, "I think everybody should get **rich and famous** and do everything they ever dreamed of so they can see that it's **not** the answer."

West is becoming very much interested in meditation, and other eastern treasures. There is a reason why the west is so interested in spirituality. The East was also interested in meditation when the East was rich; this must be understood.

"Whenever a country becomes poor, it loses contact with all spirituality. Whenever a country becomes poor outwardly, it becomes unaware of the inner poverty," said Osho. When India was rich, many people were interested in finding the true self. India was known as the land of the seekers. There was an effort to meditate. India was once known as the golden bird. Constant plundering and loot by Islamic rulers and British brought the country to its knees. For centuries, we were searching for outer freedom. We forgot to look inside. Millions of people died in the fight for freedom. Even after freedom, the politicians kept looting the public money.

It is not shocking that West is most interested in the eastern practices than the east. West is the most affluent. They are bound to see sooner or later what Jim Carrey saw.

If you have to worry about how you will earn your next day food, meditation is not for you. If you don't have to worry about food, clothing, and shelter, you are rich enough to see inside. You don't have to become a CEO and then realize that the quest was all in vain. You don't have to repeat the same mistake that world has made for thousands of years.

14. Meditation is not for the poor

You can never convince a poor person to meditate. Meditation is for the well-to-do.

You can understand why it will be almost impossible for the poor to meditate. Meditation doesn't give you any belief. It doesn't give you any promise. Religions teach us all the absurdities. It gives us false faith. Meditation doesn't give you any faith. It's your own little personal experience which promises you nothing.

You can never sit quietly until you are still hungry. You cannot sit quietly if water is leaking from your cracked ceiling. This is the very reason why most spiritual organizations focus on the rich or at least well-to-do people. They are aware that external poverty will never make these persons realize that they are poor inside.

Why Nobody Wants to Go to Church Anymore is a book written by Joani Schultz and Thom Schultz. The author says, "The American church is shrinking...fast. God-loving people are leaving in droves, and everything that attracted them in the past simply doesn't work anymore." Somewhere between 4,000 and 7,000 churches close their doors every year in the west.

Rich pray only when they have some personal problems, else there is no need for any faith or divine intervention. Now come to India. Here the churches are mushrooming. Poor are getting attracted to the concept of heaven and grace of God. In fact, there are a lot of benefits given to the lower income groups including lower fees for Christian students in Christian schools and lower fees for Christian patients in Christian hospitals. This is what the poor want. Once they will be rich, the fearful will still remain but their children will start questioning the faith.

Many Indians in anticipation for a good education for their children are getting baptised. A rich will not convert to Christianity to get those benefits. Poor make a good argument that 'what can Hinduism give me'? Being a Christian, i can give a better education to my kid'. You cannot disagree with such an argument. They are 100% correct when they say so. Some religions have a certain appeal for the poor while some are for the well off. Religions designed for the poor, are under threat since the world will slowly become rich and it will not need those religions at all.

You will never see a beggar in the temple. He will be sitting outside it. They are too poor to pray. They are too hungry to meditate. Their basic goal is bread, shelter, and clothing. None of these words say - **Pray**.

Poor want cheap schools and hospitals. That is why you will see so many Christian schools and hospitals. You will never see meditation halls by Christianity. That doesn't create any value in the eye of a poor. What does poor achieve by meditation? He can never understand.

There is a reason why some religion still wants poverty in the world. That is there sweet spot and hope. If poverty from the world goes, nobody will aspire for heaven after death. They will be living heaven-like on this earth.

Have you noticed that the religious conversion happens for both the poor and the rich? Christianity and Mohammedanism are religions of the poor. Poor in India willingly convert to Christianity. A poor person aims to be rich. If he cannot be rich on earth, he wants to go to a rich man's heaven for sure. On the contrary, rich Americans and Russians are converting to Buddhism and Hinduism. Religion has a certain appeal for both poor and rich.

When the west was poor, Christianity was the dominant force. Now that the west is rich, Christianity is dying there. Western religions have nothing to give to the rich. They were born to rule and exploit the poor. For a rich and educated man, western religion makes little sense. You all must have seen so many spiritual leaders heading towards the west. From Vivekananda to Paramhansa to Osho to Sri Sri Ravishankar, all have found a great following in the west. Their message was not to substitute the present religion with a new religion but to give people something beyond that. Meditation and yoga are such practices which are now widely accepted across the West.

In fact, when Indian Prime minister proposed the International yoga day, a record number of 177 countries agreed to the proposal. This established the International Day of Yoga for observance by the United Nations on 21 June each year.

Indian practices are beyond religious beliefs. They are designed for humans and not robots. You don't need to have faith in anybody to practise. This is your own journey.

The world is coming towards organic farming. It is time we focus on the organic growth of human beings. We don't need religions and beliefs to lead a good life. We don't have to worry about what happens after death.

But sadly, our training is of the mind. Our education is for the mind. Our ambitions, desires are the outcome of the mind and can only be fulfilled by the mind. Everyone wants us to become somebody. Our parents, society, teachers, education is all designed to make us something. There is an innate assumption that we are nothing and have to achieve something or become something to get recognition from society. I remember my college professors blaming students that we come here only to get a good job. We have made colleges as placement agencies. They are correct.

But we have not made college a placement agency. This is the very basis of our existence - to become somebody. How do you become somebody? Get into good college and get a good placement. Is it not? Who cares if you have a degree of IIM or any other top college unless you have high salary packages unless you have a big car or a big house or a classy designation? Who cares about anything else?

The mind gives you so much. People have used the mind to become Kings, Prime ministers, Presidents, CEOs and what not. The mind which on one hand gave us Pope, on the other hand, gave us a scientist.

What does meditation give you? Nothing.

What did meditation give to Buddha? Buddha left his kingdom and all worldly pleasures offered by the mind. What did Jesus gain by achieving a state of no-mind? He was crucified by the people with a mind. What did Socrates achieve? He was poisoned by his own people possessed by the mind. What did Osho, Sri Sri Ravishankar, and so many spiritual gurus achieved by meditation?

A mind is always in a hurry. A mind is always ready to do something to achieve its goal. People are ready to even kill if that helps them achieve their goals. Roman kings tried killing Jesus. Osho was imprisoned in the US. People with Mind can never agree with people with no-mind.

Over 2000 years ago there was an emperor - Alexander of Mesopotamia. His only goal was to conquer the entire world. This goal motivated him to kill and massacre millions. Anyone who stood in his way was either killed or made a slave. He came very close to victory.

India stood between him and his goal. When he entered the shore of Indus, he saw a sadhu sitting beside the river. This Sadhu was sitting peacefully with his eyes closed. Alexander asked him what he was doing sitting idle. The sadhu opened his eyes and replied, "Nothing. What about you? You look very tired. Why don't you rest a bit?"

Alexander said that he is on a quest to conquer the entire world and has no time to waste. Both laughed at each other's reply thinking other to be insane. Alexander would have thought, "What a fool! He is wasting his life without any goal."

Mind and meditation cannot exist together. Meditation simply means no-hurry. There is nothing to be done. There is nothing to be achieved. A meditative mind is without any desires, without any expectations. With mind, most men cannot achieve a meditative state. The mind will not let you sit quietly. It will keep pushing you liked it pushed Hitler. It will keep you moving like Alexander. The mind is 'I' while meditation is losing the 'I'.

How many of us want to be a Buddha? Who wants to be a nobody? Everybody wants to go higher on the ladder of ambitions. People sacrifice their whole life to become somebody. Alexander had the madness to conquer the entire world. He died a highly disappointed man. Why? Because this is how the mind goes on leading you farther and farther: It goes on telling you, 'Just a few miles more'. Alexander couldn't even reach his home before he died at the tender age of thirty-three.

Look at all the people on the streets in the morning. They are in a hurry. Stress is our own creation. Stress and depression are part of our lifestyle. Stress is the root cause of so many illnesses around the world. In fact, 90% of our entire visits to the doctor can be attributed to stress. One life theory is also responsible for this rat race. We are in a hurry to achieve. It is such a proud moment for people to be CEO before 40. Even in the 30s, people are planning for their retirement.

Time has been made linear by Christianity. It's all surrounding Christ - before Christ and after Christ. Christ was the big bang for the world.

In India, we don't even know when Ram or Krishna walked the planet. We don't even know if they ever walked. There was no concept of time for the east. Time was never linear for us. Time was always circular like the spokes of a wheel. Birth and death were cyclical.

Time is never linear in nature. Look at the seasons. Summer goes and winter follows. Again summer comes. Time is not linear, it's cyclical. The whole universe is a standstill. Earth is rotating on its axis from last 4 billion years. It's not going anywhere. The stars, the planets are all revolving around the same axis. Everything thing in the space is round. Nothing is linear in nature.

Time cannot be linear, but the west has made it linear. East believes in many lives. We are not going anywhere. We are born and then we die and we again take birth. This is a cyclical process. West believed in one life, hence the need for time. Time is needed to do great things as only limited life was there. Only 70 or 80 years to live. There is an urgency to do something great. East was able to get into meditation because it didn't care for the time. Alexander couldn't rest as there was no time to rest.

A newborn is closer to real nature of human. Look how beautiful she is. Even the newborn of animals. When they grow up, they lose their grace. They start losing their natural rhythm. They no longer laugh spontaneously, they no longer cry spontaneously. A child is in the state of meditation or no-mind. Once it gets the concept of 'I', grace is slowly lost. There is no grace in the eyes of a man driven by the mind.

15. Mind your mind

A mind is your past constantly trying to control your present and your future. It is the dead past which goes on controlling the alive present.

How the mind does go on doing that? The mind fills us with fear. Remember the last time when you wanted to take a new route to work and the mind gave you a lot of explanations as to why you shouldn't take that route? It makes up arguments like - "maybe you will take longer time through that route" or "maybe there will be more traffic there", or "maybe you will get lost and end up taking more time". Such excuses are of a mind.

The mind loves repetition and certainty. If you do the old thing, you can be 100% sure if it will work or not. You can be efficient with repetition. Haven't you heard - "Practice make a man perfect"? Why do you want to become perfect? Perfection means that whatever you are doing becomes effortless. Isn't it?

Remember the age-old habits. We are advised to make good habits and leave the bad ones. Habits are mind's way of repetition. The mind likes repetition. It wants you to stick to old habits. New ones are very difficult to build especially the so-called good ones. Waking up early is a very difficult habit. Starting anything new is difficult. A mind has certain inertia.

When you achieve experience and consistency, your mind can move here and there easily. Let me explain. Suppose you are going on the same daily route to work. You don't have to be aware. Your body can work like a robot and take you to your destination. You can drift away with your mind to any place and time. You are not needed at the present moment.

Now imagine you taking a new route to the office today. What will happen? You have to be aware and present on the road. You cannot afford to miss any turn. You will be thinking less and be more attentive. The mind will be in the backseat. It will be working alongside to register the path for the next drive.

To tame the mind, we have to really understand how it works. Unless we understand that, we will never address its challenges.

A mind is always looking for a trigger. The moment it gets a trigger, it races off. There is no stopping to it. Let me explain. I show you a picture of a tiger i have recently taken at a zoo. Immediately your mind will trigger memories of yours which are either concerned with a zoo or a tiger. Anything interesting which happened to you will immediately start running. In case i am still around, you will start telling me the story of what happened that day. Remember i didn't ask you to tell me anything. It is happening spontaneously.

We ask people to listen more and talk less. How is it possible? Their mind is creating so many triggers that they will keep interrupting others. They cannot quite their mind. They are getting so many thoughts that they are forced to speak.

If you get one thought, the mind will not stop there. It will give you another memory. Then another. It's like a trail of thoughts. One thought creates an automatic trigger for the next one. Anything you see, hear, touch can create memories. You might have often noticed this when we are doing something very mundane like driving or reading. We suddenly realize that well we were not aware of what was happening in present. We were almost gone into the trail of thoughts.

A mind can never be quiet. That is its very nature. You cannot achieve peace of mind. A mind is like a small kid. It only knows to run around here and there. If you try to control it, it revolts. Try to forcibly control your mind once and you will know what i am talking about. One good example i can remember is in case you have heard a song many times a day and now you are writing an exam. What happens? That song keeps playing in your mind. I have tried to stop that disturbance so that i can think of the answers to the question paper but the mind doesn't hear. It is almost impossible to quieten the mind. That song keeps playing in the back of my mind.

Well, there is a way though. What happens when you are doing something really interesting? Say you are playing cricket or watching a movie or watching a favourite sitcom? Have you noticed that your mind is nowhere to be found? At the same time compare this with an activity which you don't like for example - studies. Now you forcibly sit on the study table for reading. What happens is for nobody to guess. You get distracted. You spend time sharpening the pencil, finding the right notebook, highlighter etc. You are not at all focused. Why? Because you are not enjoying what you are doing.

The mind will intervene constantly in such situations. On the contrary, find a kid who loves studies. An even better example will be a scientist. Look closely when he or she is working. He is so concentrated that he doesn't even have time to look up. When you are enjoying something, the mind is not there. You are totally lost. Basically, the "I" is not present. When the "I" is not there, how can the mind exist?

When you are watching your favourite movie, you are lost in that. That is why in the movie theatres the lights are dimed. There should be nothing which should distract you. Imagine you are watching the movie in a theatre with lights on. You will get distracted very easily. If someone is moving around, popcorn guy passes by; there is a great chance of distraction. If you get distracted, the experience of the movie will never be that great.

Remember that guy in the back seat talking on the phone. Such a small thing can ruin your whole experience. That is why we are constantly asked to keep our phone on silent and not to speak loudly when the movie is playing. No distraction should be there.

Hobbies are the new trend. Everyone wants to have a hobby they can do in part-time. Why? The simple reason is to get rid of the mind, to forget oneself. Hobby is simply an activity which you enjoy doing. Someone loves to read, some like to sleep some extra hours, some love gardening. Most therapists and psychologists will recommend people suffering from depression to take up a hobby. The hobby will keep you engaged and let you forget yourself.

When you read a book, you forget yourself. You forget your worries. That is why it is so enjoyable to read good fiction. It is not that people who have read 100 fiction books will be more intelligent. They simply got an experience what it feels like to forget one and go into a fantasy world created by the author. Besides this, there is not a single rupee benefit out of reading fiction. It's like watching a movie only more intense. Why? Because here not only you have to read but also use your mind for imagination. You have to visualize what is happening in the plot.

The more we engage the mind into something, the less the time mind has to drift and think about your problems. We drink to suppress the mind.

16. Present is a "Present"

Being in the present is a blessing. Probably that is why we called it "Present". Depression is caused when we are not in present; we are either in the past or in some unknown future. We regret the past. We want to become something or we want to achieve something. We are always anticipating a future.

People who remain in the present can never get depression. A small child is never depressed because he or she is totally in the present. He is living moment by moment with no anticipation of the future and no regrets of the past.

Depression happens when our mind is focussed on the future. A mind is always either in the past or in the future. When mind is not focused on anything in the present, it has a habit of moving. A mind cannot sit idle. When you watch a movie or play a game that you really like, the mind is no more. Although it is a forced one, concentration simply means no mind. You are so focussed on something that your mind has stopped all movements.

The more we run after desires, the more we are prone to depression. The more we are unwilling to accept to what *is*, we run for an imaginative what *can be*. Not being content with what you have is a direct reason for constant displeasure.

Tension, stress, anxiety, and depression are attributes of a mind. Our mind is an outcome of our conditioning and the society we live in. Depression is also one of the outcomes of a materialistic world. We have embraced a materialistic world with both hands. Education is also one of the reasons behind depression. When we were kids, we were stressed in anticipation of good marks. Not even good marks but to be also better than others. If I get 90% and rest of the class gets 95%, that's terrible for me.

Our whole education system is a big mess. It is designed to create all these mental problems from a very young age. It is no wonder that suicide is among the top three reasons for death among the age group of 12-18. Our children are committing suicides. Imagine the state of the mind of a child that he is willing to kill himself. At such a young age!

Are we not happy? Is our lust for materialism ever going to end? We are stressed and anxious because we are running a rat race. And not just any rats race but a self-created one. We anticipate becoming a VP by 35, an MD by 40, CEO by 45, and finally retirement by 55. That is not you. If you have goals similar to the above, that is your conditioning speaking. Who told you that becoming a CEO should be the ultimate goal? Who told you that becoming CEO will give you real happiness? Why do we love to live in such a hypothetical and fake way?

I am still surprised that a body for which the ultimate truth is death, why are we so adamant in achieving something great? What happened to all those great leaders of men? What happened to all the kings and queens? What happened to all the CEOs? The present generation is suffering because of their decisions while those greats are all lying in their graves.

When we are running this anticipated future sprints, we are bound to get stressed. We are bound to miss one or the other targets. The educated are sadder than the poor. No poor are lining outside therapists or psychiatrists. Almost half of the world is suffering from mental diseases. We are suffering our own mind.

Stress comes when we don't know how to manage the present. Isn't it? Suppose you are working on a project and some major escalation happens. How well can you handle such a present situation? Our inability to handle the present causes stress. In fact, globally 33% of the adults are suffering from hypertension. Another 20% have hypertension but aren't aware of it. If we add the numbers, more than 50% of our adult population is suffering from hypertension. Hypertension leads to 1000 deaths every single day across the world. For those of you don't understand hypertension, it is closely related to stress. Although there are many other reasons still one cannot rule stress from the picture.

There is a real-life case that I heard a few years back. So what happened is this. There is a successful IT professional working as a senior manager. He is earning a good amount of money and has a happy family and life. He loves his present job and his colleagues love him too. Things are going smooth. One day he gets an invitation from his college to attend the yearly Alumni meet. He was excited to revisit the old memories with his family. He reached the college on the day and met a lot of old colleagues and professors.

He was very happy visiting the hostel room, hostel mess and favourite hangout places. He met some friends who were now directors and vice presidents in big companies and probably earning more than double of what he was. He was very impressed by their success.

When he reached home, something inside him was not well. He was not feeling happy. He didn't understand what happened but he was feeling uneasy. He was not happy hearing that his colleagues are now more successful than him. A life which was going so well suddenly looks dull and clumsy. He was jealous of his colleagues who were now earning better packages. He decided to switch job anticipating higher salary and designation. Soon he got an offer from a company but the location was not his present one. He had to relocate to a new city which meant that he had to leave his family behind as his kids were in the middle of their school terms. Wife obviously cannot accompany him as kids are to be looked after.

Now, this guy has relocated with a higher package to a new place without family. He has a higher package and a better designation but now his kids will not be with him till the next 6 months.

This is no hypothetical story. There was an actual case study done where it was found that after alumni meet, job switches increased considerably. This research was done with the students of a very reputed Indian college.

What changes in your life before and after the alumni meet? Same life was looking so much better before and now it looks depressing. The reason is simple. We want to define success in terms of how society measures it - in terms of power (money + position). More the power, more you get respected. We want to look successful to others. If others don't think I am successful, that is it for me. I will start looking for more success.

"An undying smile is a sign of success," says spiritual leader Sri Sri Ravishankar.

Why is it so difficult to live in the present?

Look at your life. We have become almost mechanical. We are living in repetition.

Mind is always either in the past or the future. A mind can never be in the present. If you are in the present, the mind is not there. When the mind is there, it is not possible to be in the present. We enjoy sports so much is because it keeps us in the present moment. When we are in the present, work is not work. Work becomes play. That is why we are fresh even after playing a game of badminton or any other sports but we get tired by sitting at one place for the same amount of time. Although we spend a lot of energy still a lot of energy is saved because the mind didn't travel.

The mind has been troubling people from time eternal. In order to get rid of the troublemaker i.e. our mind, people leave their families and go to ashrams and Himalayas. Buddha left his palace in order to find the meaning of life. There is nothing in a Himalaya as such, but people want to run away from this world. They want to run away from anything that distracts them. What distracts us? Isn't it our world – our neighbours, our family, and our office colleagues? In fact, people take leaves from office to relax and get their peace of mind.

In order to get permanent peace of mind, people try to run away from everything that causes distractions to their minds. Some saint has even called women a door to hell. Why? It is actually very easy to understand.

This guy must have been so distracted seeing a woman that he blamed women for his rising sexuality. That is what weak people do. They blame others for their problems. It is easier to blame women for provoking your desires and bringing sexual thoughts.

Muslims want their females to wear a burqa on the similar logic. Men know that they cannot control their sexual urges and thoughts on seeing a female. It is better to cover their women up! This will prevent such desires from popping up in their minds.

Since we cannot control our mind, we suggest all these stupid ideas to others. Men are ready to blame the short dress of a woman for arousing them. Some men are so deprived of sex that they are even willing to become human bombs simply in anticipation that they will get 72 virgins in heaven!

Once upon a time, there lived a king. He had a beautiful and intelligent queen. Queen was always spiritually inclined but King was too busy in the materialistic needs. When the King became old, he decided to give up everything and go to the forest. Without informing anyone, one night the king left the kingdom and went to some unknown place.

After a few months, the queen came to know the whereabouts of the king. She went to a nearby jungle and saw the king living an ordinary life of a hermit. She decided to test her husband. She disguised herself as a saint and went in front of him. The king greeted the saint. The saint said, "You don't look like a person born as a hermit. I have also never seen you here. Who are you?"

The king said, "I was a king. I have now renounced the world and settled in this forest. You must have been really tired of travelling across this dense jungle. Why don't you spend some time in my hut?"

The saint said, "You seem to claim that you have renounced everything but i don't see that here. What have you really renounced? All the materialistic things that you left behind were never yours. You haven't renounced anything."

The king said, "Are you talking about this stick and this pot that I carry?" Saying this, he threw the pot and the stick in the fire.

Saint said, "You haven't renounced everything, yet"

The king looked at his small hut and put that on fire. He looked at the saint for approval but the saint again said, "You haven't renounced everything."

The king said, "I only have these clothes that i still carry." saying this, he threw the clothes into the nearby fire. The king was now standing naked.

The saint again said, "Still you haven't renounced everything."

The king was furious. He said, "What do i have now that i haven't forsaken? I have given up my entire kingdom, my wife, my children, my hut and even my clothes. Why do you keep saying that i haven't renounced everything? What is left now with me? I only have this body left. Let me jump into the fire and renounce this as well."

The saint asked the king to stop and said, "You are ready to destroy this body but when are you planning to renounce the mind? You haven't renounced your mind. Unless you have done that, what have you really renounced?"

Where can you leave your dirty mind? No matter wherever you go, you cannot escape your mind. Your mind will follow you. Your anger will follow you into the jungles. Your fears will follow you inside the Himalayan caves.

A mind is a bundle of thoughts. Thoughts are dependent on 'I'. Even in your dream, you are always there. 'I' is never missing even in your dream. Other actors can come and go but you are always there. 'I' is base of the thoughts and the mind. If we want to get rid of the mind, we have to get rid of the "I".

For a moment, just forget about your past: where you were born, whether you are male or female, whether you have the money or not, whether you are educated or not, whether you have a family or not. Forget your past for a moment. What will you think about? For a moment, you can feel what it feels like to get into a state of no-mind. Your "I" has been forgotten at that moment, what can you think about? Your very ego must be destroyed to avoid overthinking!

Only when we get rid of the mind, we can come to the present. We can attain happiness. We can lead a stress-free life.

17. Social Media and Anxiety

I still remember the day when one of my college friends introduced me to Orkut. It was something new. You could find people, share messages and what not. Before that, our life was very simple. Opinions were shared in groups. We were the consumers of data. We were only concerned about our closed ones and family. There was hardly any anxiety because of what people beyond your circle are doing or saying. There was no way to know unless someone tells you. If you had opinions, you would discuss it with your friends over a cup of tea and that's it. Those were simpler days.

It's not that we were not jealous of our friends and family. We had all the emotions. But i feel that those negative emotions lasted really for a short span of time and we used to move on with life. The internet has come down heavily on the masses. There are now so many billion dollar businesses which are purely running on the internet. The most impactful of all is the invention of social media. We now have Facebook, Blogs, LinkedIn, Instagram, Quora, WhatsApp, Twitter and many more. Millions of people across the globe are spending hours and hours every day on these sites. Each site is competing with others to get that extra time from the users. And do you know what the best part is? It is FREE!

There is no doubt that these social media is corrupting young minds. Each application gives us a great platform to connect with the entire world. Many people have become famous and rich using these social networking sites. Never in history was it possible. But without mentioning the side effects of social media, it would be little injustice. Some social media applications are designed simply for marketing and wasting our time.

I am not suggesting that technology or social media is a bad thing, but we are addicted. Any form of addiction is bad. This is what the president of the largest social media site has to say. He says, "The thought process that went into building these applications was how to consume as much of your time and (un) conscious attention as possible. And that means that we have to give you a dopamine hit (updates, likes, comments, and friend requests) once in a while. Most social media founders knew about this human psychology and they did it anyway. They exploited the human psychology of longing for appreciation."

Chamath Palihapitiya, one of the social media developer says, "Consumer internet businesses are about exploiting (human) psychology and that is one where we have to move fast, because people are predictable, and we have to figure out how to psychologically manipulate you as fast as possible and give you that dopamine hit. We have done it brilliantly at Facebook, Instagram, WhatsApp, Twitter, and WeChat. If you feed the beast, it will destroy you and the fabric of our society. If we push back on it, we have a chance to control it."

Our mobiles have become like gambling machines. Social media has become like a slot machine. Every time we pull the lever we want something good to happen. Some likes, comments, messages. This is practically unethical as we are not doing it consciously. Someone has learned about this gap in the human mind and exploiting us to death. They are now using it to manipulate elections. The more frequently your mobile buzzes, the more frequently you become conditioned. It is leading to these addictive problems that the whole world is facing.

We are more distracted than ever. Spiritual guru Dandapani says, "People find it difficult to concentrate because we are never taught how to concentrate, and we don't practice concentration. How can we be good at something if we don't practice it?" Day in day out we are being distracted from everything including mobile phones to the internet to social media to television shows. It is no wonder that the present generation is also the most distracted one. We are practicing distraction day in day out, no wonder we are becoming good at it.

We are not paying money every time we pull the lever of this slot machine, but we are investing even more valuable things: our time, our peace of mind, and our attention span. Again, mobile too is not a bad tool. It's an excellent tool which makes our life simpler. It helps us save a lot of time and money in communicating with others. But we are addicted. If you feel you are not, don't check your social media account for the next 7 days. Can you do the same with your mobile? You are allowed to call and text people only if required. Rest of the time, your data will be off. What do you think? If you are feeling uneasy, chances are you are addicted. Addicted to the short-term dopamine feedback loop, we are destroying how society works.

We are spending a staggering amount of hours every day. Our friend circle is reducing to social media friends. We now have a compulsive habit of sharing all our life's happy moments on social media. When we now travel to any place for tourism, our focus now is to get a perfect photo of our social media accounts. Isn't it? Females are little ahead in this race to get that perfect picture. We need to give something to our followers!

The negative emotions which earlier might be triggered rarely, now are triggered every day. Feelings of jealousy, envy, anxiety, sadness are now triggered every single day. With thousands of connections on social media, we get to see happy stories every day. Someone is going on an exotic foreign trip. Someone is enjoying with his family in a resort. Someone is getting married while others are becoming parents. Someone has got an award or a promotion, while others are partying on weekends. Someone has bought a new expensive car or a house. Not only our colleagues, now we can follow celebrities on these social media sites. We are now getting fitness and travels goals from them.

Understand the psyche that is working here. Inventors of social media know how a human mind works. They must have involved some psychologists and psychiatrists in their development team. People long for appreciation. Haven't you heard people saying "Public Praise / Private Criticism"? People like to show-off, be it some talent or money. Money has a compulsive feeling. If you have money, you want to tell others you have else what is the use? We want to buy expensive brands not that they are super comfortable, but because people will know that you are rich. Our ego inflates with money. If someone not matching your richness insults you, what happens? Your ego is really hurt. How can a poor man insult me?

When we share anything on social media, we are only looking for positive affirmations. We want appreciations and likes. We enjoy that. While we like appreciation, there is another angle as well. We like to show-off. We like to show that our life is so good. We are living a dream life that others should be a little jealous like we were when they shared their beautiful pictures. There is a competition going on in our minds. We are now judging people based on their social media accounts.

We are playing directly in the hands of these social media and the increase in the users of these tools is direct proof that the human mind is so predictable. People can be fooled easily these days. Anything can be shared and instantly believed. Fake news can be spread easily. Social media has become really influential. Everybody is now a writer. Everybody can now share their opinion. It's all about getting viral now. All these do give us a lot of anxiety.

In fact, now we have a new word called "Instagramxiety". Instagramxiety is to describe the negative impacts of Instagram. Social media is now being blamed for degrading mental health of the people. "Seeing friends constantly on holiday or enjoying nights out can make young people feel like they are missing out while others enjoy life," stated the #StatusOfMind report (based on a survey done in the UK).

61% of all Instagram users are between the age of 18 and 34. Millions of millennials are spending at least 2 hours per day, often more, on Instagram. Here are some of the key signs of social media anxiety:

- Inner tension and worry about what people are doing on social media, and if you measure up

- Agitation, anxiety especially when checking the app

- Fear of missing out (FOMO)

- A Constant need for more likes and comments

- Feeling disappointment on seeing more likes and comments on the feeds of a friend

- Constantly feeling if you are good enough

- Anxiety, if unable to access social media for some time

These are some of the common symptoms most of us face on social media. As i said earlier, life was much simpler before the advent of social media. We were satisfied with our life. Anxiety if at all, was short-lived. These apps are now causing stress and it is a deliberate intrusion in our lives. We don't want to be stressed and addicted but we are now slaves to these apps. Mobile is now our new master. No wonder we call it smart phones.

So, what is the solution to this? Can we let social media play with our mind?

"First of all, just realize that many people who post all that great stuff on Facebook have a normal life just like you and me but they only put the good stuff on Facebook. If your life is not as awesome as some of the people you see on Facebook, it is not going to get any better by sitting there obsessing over it. You have to get out and enjoy your real life, not your social media "life" because that is not real life. If you are having trouble doing this or you just need to talk to someone, there are people who can help you with this. You do not have to have an appointment or even leave your home to do it. Talk to an online therapist or counselor now and you can feel better by tomorrow," said Sarah Fader founder of Stigma Fighters.

There's no shortage of evidence that loneliness, social anxiety, and social isolation can cause excessive use of social networking sites in young people. For example, a study of university students in the UK found that real life social interaction was negatively associated with excessive use of Twitter, and loneliness was a significant factor that mediated this relationship [13], so it's clear that many people use social networking sites, in general, to relieve themselves of their loneliness.

Most of us have to really understand that social media is not giving us any benefit. It is now all about marketing. The more time we spend on these sites, the more money these social media founders make. It's all about advertisements. It is not free! You are paying them with your precious time and data. We all are using social media now from the last 15-20 years. Introspect as to what have you really gained out of it? Do you not feeling sad and anxious seeing the happy life of others?

Understand that our mind likes repetition. It doesn't want to do new things. Getting out of social media addiction can be tough, but we have to do it. We have to reduce our time online. It is definitely possible.

So, what is the solution? If someone explains to you the harmful effects of social media, you will not understand. It is so difficult. I have seen people drinking cigarettes even though there such disturbing images and warning on the packet. They cannot stop. The only way of change is awareness. The only way is self-realization. Unless you yourself see the efficacy of using social media, it will be too difficult to use. You have been using social media from so many years. What have you really gained by investing so much time in it? If you don't know the answer, your realization should be immediate. You have no reason to stick to social media and spend hours and hours on it.

Self-realization is the only solution. If it hasn't come yet, wait for the day when it will strike you. Unless you realize that social media is causing more anxiety than happiness, you will automatically stop using it. If you are holding stones and thinking about it like diamonds, no amount of cajoling and logic will make you throw away those rocks. The moment you realize that you are actually holding rocks, you will drop them automatically.

18. Get set go!

There is an interesting theory in Christian theology. In Genesis 2:17, God said: *"but from the tree of the knowledge of good and evil you shall not eat, for in the day that you eat from it you will surely die."*

Adam and Eve lived happily in the Garden of Eden. God and Jesus came and talked to them. There were many trees in the garden. God said Adam and Eve could eat fruit from all the trees but one. God warned them that if they ate from the tree they would die. It was the tree of good and evil. If they ate fruit (fruit of knowledge) from that tree, they would know what was good and what was bad. They would have to leave the Garden of Eden. If they did not eat it, they could always stay in the Garden of Eden.

One day Satan disguised as a snake came to Eve and tempted her to eat the fruit of knowledge. Eve and Adam consumed the fruit. They lost all the innocence. Now they were aware of what was good and bad. They got the knowledge. They got a mind. When God came to see them, they hid behind the trees of the garden. Feeling of guilt and nakedness overpowered them.

They later admitted to the God that they ate from the tree of knowledge. They were banished from the Garden of Eden into a life of sufferings. Whether true or untrue, this story is beautiful.

Who is the Satan and what is the fruit of knowledge? I saw some people debating if the fruit was actually an apple or a pomegranate. It really doesn't matter. It was the fruit of knowledge. It was a fruit to lose your innocence. You can no more live with the Gods. You can no more be peaceful and happy. You have gained the knowledge of good and bad. You have gained the knowledge to become a mind. You become the 'I'.

Knowledge destroys innocence. The Feeling of 'I' destroys the innocence. Jesus says, "Unless you become like children, you cannot enter into my kingdom of God." Children are not aware of their body. A child is standing naked - no one feels the nakedness because the child is unaware of the body. Adam and Eve were naked. When they ate the fruit of knowledge, they became aware. They became aware of guilt, lust, greed etc. They came to realize that they were naked. In the bible knowledge is a sin. Unless they become like children, they cannot enter the kingdom of God.

If you look at our education system, each and every child has to go through it. It's mandatory for a good life, they say. Instead of the fruit of knowledge, we now have schools, colleges, and universities. The kid now learns good and bad in the institutions. Children learn moral values. They are told what is bad and what should not be done. The fruit of knowledge is forced down their throat. They have no choice. Each child was born innocent, is made non-innocent. Now once they grow up, most of us struggle to become innocent again. It was not easy for Adam and Eve and it no more easy even today. Innocence through wisdom is the only way out. Buddha took 29 years before he realized this. He took another 6 years to attain that innocence back.

This world values knowledge. This world needs knowledge. You cannot exist without knowledge. You are not valuable without knowledge to help the world move forward. Children cannot help move this world forward. Knowledge is a necessary evil, you cannot escape it. This world is a strange place. To be successful in this world, you need to have knowledge.

To transcend the knowledge of good and the bad, you have to once again realize that good and bad don't exist. They exist as two sides of the same coin. There is no division. Innocence can also be because of ignorance. A child is ok to be naked as he or she is not aware of the body. But real innocence is that once you have the knowledge of good and bad and yet you can still transcend that. Adam and Eve were sent to become mature. They were given knowledge so that they can transcend it and regain that innocence but this time with awareness. Transcending the mind is the goal.

Remember how the moral science book defined a human being? They call us a social animal. An Animal! Why Animal? Because animals need to be trained. They have to be told what is good and bad. If left alone, they cannot be moral and good to society. There is an inherent problem here. In posing those moralities, we have caused more destruction to the world than ever. In defining who is normal and who is not, psychiatry has ruined millions of lives. In deciding who is right and who is wrong, we have had so many endless wars. In deciding whose religion is better, we are still fighting with each other.

Science has divided everything into good and bad. Good brain cells and Bad brain cells. Good bacteria and Bad bacteria. Good cholesterol and bad cholesterol. Anger is bad while compassion is good. Hatred is bad while love is good. If you have ups and downs you are bipolar (not normal) but if you are a flat line (you are normal). Now, we have started calling Ego as bad. All these are absolutely absurd theories but we believe in the knowledge that is given to us. Now we even have good terrorist and bad terrorist. What is this? If you are a terrorist and you attack my enemy, you are good for me.

It doesn't work this way. All the negatives and positives are of the mind. If you get angry, that is who you are. There is no label needed. This is your energy. Anger is always there. That is who you are. You simply needed a trigger. Nobody can bring anger in you. It was always there. For example, you can switch on and off the bulb in a room. But for this on and off to take place, electricity must be present all the time. A mind is anger. A mind is lust. A mind is greed. A greedy mind cannot transform a greedy mind into a non-greedy mind. It's not possible. No matter how hard you try, you will get angry.

Acceptance of your energies is the way to transcend it. Accept your mind. Accept your feelings of lust, greed, anger, guilt.

Microorganisms and animals have been the oldest inhabitants of this planet. Humans are the latest life on the planet, yet we never see animals depressed. We may see them depressed in a zoo or a cage but when left alone, there is no depression or anxiety. You will never see them complaining or questioning the meaning of life. They have no concept of God.

There is something unique about humans. French philosopher Jean-Paul Sartre says that man lives as if he has been thrown into the world. We behave as we are living here without our consent. There are frustration and anguish as a result.

Animals act purely based on their instinct. They are not trying to become anyone else. A fish doesn't want to become a bird. They are simply as they are. This is probably one of the main reasons why humans are mentally disturbed. We are never satisfied as who we are. We want to get rid of something. We want to add something to our 'I'. We are always comparing us to others. We have role models. I am sure even those role models will have others as role models. We are always trying to become someone else.

If we succeed in becoming someone, our ego gets inflated. That is why we like to add Dr. in front of our names. Psychiatrists did everything possible to add the 'Dr.' word in front of their names. We love to flaunt our achievements. Without them, we feel inferior. The same inferiority kicks in when we fail in the eyes of society. We feel depressed. We feel useless.

Spiritual leader Sri Sri Ravishankar says, "The sadness in you is there because there is a thorn of desire that is stuck in your heart. And when you don't notice it, it turns into cynicism, sarcasm, frustration, and anger. And if you notice it and manage to pull it out, you will be fulfilled with joy, enthusiasm, contentment, and compassion."

Happiness is our very nature. What overshadows this happiness is 'I want this', or, 'I want that', 'I want something'. This is what brings anxiety and puts away happiness. If you take any of the above sentences and start removing the words, you will understand what i am saying.

Example: Take the sentence 'I want something'. Remove the 'I' from that. What is left? We are left with 'Want something'. Now selectively remove 'Want'. We are left with 'Something'. Where is the stress now? Who is stressed? Where are the negative thoughts in this? Stress is a direct outcome of an anxious mind. 'I' and 'Wants' are our mental issues. When we sleep we forget the 'I' and the 'wants'. That is why sleep feels so good. That is why we feel refreshed after a good night sleep. Sleep helps us return to that innocence.

I have often heard people having depression saying that they don't like to get off the bed. They love to sleep as it is a respite from their anxiety. Drugs and alcohol also work in a similar way. They help us forget 'I' and our 'wants'. What more proof do you need to understand this? I once heard a beautiful story behind the words – illness, and wellness. If you look carefully, the two words have been formed with a great message. Illness starts with a strong feeling of 'I'. Wellness starts with the feeling of '**We**'. The stronger we stick to 'I' the more illnesses we invite.

Psychiatry is not interested in the reasons for your anxiety. They don't care 'WHY' you are depressed. They are trained to give you a pill for every ill. If you can find a psychiatrist who can talk you through your problem, you can visit him or her. But sadly, most psychiatrists are only concerned with your symptoms. They are not concerned 'Why' you have those symptoms.

I am not suggesting that by losing 'I' and 'Wants' you should become a saint. No. That is not my intention. You can still do whatever you want to do. You don't have to leave your family or house. You have simply become Egoless. You have to be like a child. Understand that fulfilling even the highest desires, will not satisfy you. Your mind is just a vagabond, a wandering. It is never at a point. It is always going, moving, reaching, but never at any point. That is also the reason why we find it difficult to concentrate. A mind cannot concentrate. That is its very nature. The very structure of the mind is movement.

You can try another small experiment. You can close your eyes to this experiment. Imagine that you have had an accident and you have lost your entire memory to date. You don't remember anything. You have lost your name, your family, your education, your job. Your entire past in wiped out. Not even a trace is left behind. Now sit in this state for a few minutes. Your mind and thoughts will come in and will distract you. Don't worry. Again repeat the same sentences and sit with your eyes closed. Does this exercise as long as you want? Look at your state of mind now. How do you feel? Do you feel any better?

Society and your family have been instrumental in creating your mind. If you would have left alone from your childhood, you would have been much better off. For the rest of our life, we do everything to satisfy society. We marry, we give birth, we do a 9 to 6 job, and we buy cars, go for foreign trips, all to satisfy the society.

Society has given us a definition of success. More the money you earn, the more successful you are. These things have ruined our mind. We feel depressed when we are not able to satisfy our parents and society.

There can be genuine cases of depression and anxiety but depression always has a 'WHY'. It cannot be genetic. The whole theory of gene is bogus. That is a lie!

A lot of doctors also suggest some sort of physical activity to alleviate depression. I know that lot of us hate to go to the gym. A gym too helps us to build our 'I'. Most of us WANT to have a great body because we are suffering from low self-esteem. A great body can help your self-esteem. That is why people recommend it. You don't have to enforce your 'I'. You can learn yoga practices. In the comfort of your home, you can do a great workout and stay fit. Yoga is an ancient practice designed keeping in mind the holistic health. It works holistically on your breath, energy centres, and the body. It's a complete workout.

If you want to lose weight, you have to simply change your diet. You don't have to sweat in the gym to achieve a healthy body. I have written in detail about this topic in my book: *Why we are fat and hungry?*

One last thing before we end this book. In 2015, Deepika detailed her experience of fighting depression in an exclusive interview to NDTV saying she felt "empty" and "directionless". Psychiatry has succeeded in their plan to make the man a soulless creature. We have become a machine who are pretending and pleasing others. If we cannot do that, we feel disappointed. People who act in films and serials are bound to feel it. They are pretending most of the time. They are not being who they really are. They have to fit in the star community.

Being fake around people bring stress. Trying to please around bring stress. That is the reason why the suicide rate is very high in the film and fashion industry. That is the reason why we feel really relaxed and happy when we come back to our homes. Home is the place where we are truly ourselves. There are no cameras. You can be yourselves.

Mental illness like depression is real. There is no doubt about it. But believing that something is wrong with our brain and assuming we are diseased are big mistakes! Spirituality is the solution for the mind. Ancient practices of meditation and yoga are the natural way to deal with anxiety.

We have to understand that people having depresion don't want to talk to their loved ones. It is something which they feel might hurt you. It is also the job of the parents to create a loving environment which in not conditional. Love cannot be conditional. It cannot be that 'I love you' only if you do this.

I wish that this book helps you.

Author's Bio

Shubham Gupta is born in Kanpur, India.

He has completed his masters from the IIT.

He found a passion for reading in 2010. For next few years, he spent a lot of time reading many of the international bestsellers. He soon realized that although the knowledge shared by many western writers was plausible it was nevertheless difficult to implement.

This started his journey to spirituality.

Yoga and meditation helped him understand what many writers were missing in understanding the human mind. He took the aim to give the practical steps which readers can implement to make the transformation in their life. Life with spirituality is always dull.

He has written four self-help books (available on Amazon) till now which are focussed to give people the missing links. Other books written by him include:

1. Why we get Sick? What doctors, multinationals and pharma will never tell you!

2. Who are you? Unleash the power of the soul

3. Why we are fat and hungry? What doctors, multinationals and pharma will never tell you!

4. 5 life-changing lessons from the Near Death Experiences of others

5. There is no goal in life", are being read across the globe.

References

[1] Kiessling, Hein (2016). Faith, Unity, Discipline: The Inter-Service-Intelligence (ISI) of Pakistan. Oxford University Press. ISBN 9781849048637. Retrieved 2 October2018.

[2]https://www.everydayhealth.com/pictures/celebrities-who-have-experienced-depression/

[3,11] Miller G. Is pharma running out of brainy ideas? Science. 2010;329:502–504. [PubMed]Abbott A. Novartis to shut brain research facility. Nature. 2011;2011;480:161–162. [PubMed]

[4,12] Steven E. Hyman Psychiatric Drug Development: Diagnosing a Crisis

[5,13] Ndasauka Y, Hou J, Wang Y, Yang L et al. (2016) Excessive use of Twitter among college students in the UK: Validation of the Microblog Excessive Use Scale and relationship to social interaction and loneliness. Computers in Human Behavior, 55, 963-971.